MIXING METHODS:
QUALITATIVE AND QUANTITATIVE RESEARCH

D

Mixing Methods: qualitative and quantitative research

Edited by

Julia Brannen
Thomas Coram Research Unit
Institute of Education

ASHGATE

Published by
Ashgate Publishing Limited
Gower House
Croft Road
Aldershot
Hants
GU11 3HR
England

Ashgate Publishing Company
Suite 420
101 Cherry Street
Burlington, VT 05401-4405
USA

Ashgate website: http://www.ashgate.com

Reprinted 1993, 1994, 2003

A CIP catalogue record for the book is available from the British Library and the US Library of Congress

ISBN 1 85628 184 1

Printed in Great Britain by Biddles Limited,
Guildford and King's Lynn.

Contents

l

List of contributors

Margaret Bird is currently Staff Tutor in Education in the Open University (London region). She was formerly a Research Officer with the ILEA Research and Statistics Branch where she conducted a study of the Open College development. She has written extensively on education, and is co-author of *Education and Work* (NIACE, Leicester, 1981).

Roger Bullock is Senior Research Fellow at the Dartington Social Research Unit in the School of Applied Social Studies, University of Bristol. He has written extensively on policy-relevant research on children and young people in institutions. He is co-author of *The Chance of a Lifetime* (Weidenfeld and Nicholson, 1975), *After Grace-Teeth* (Chaucer, 1975), *Lost in Care*, (Gower, 1989).

Julia Brannen is Senior Research Officer at the Thomas Coram Research Unit, Institute of Education, University of London. Most of her research is on households and families. She is a co-editor of *Give and Take in Families* (Unwin Hyman, 1987) and co-author of *Marriages in Trouble* (Tavistock, 1982), *New Mothers at Work* (Unwin Hyman, 1988) and *Managing Mothers* (Unwin Hyman, 1991).

Alan Bryman is Reader in Social Research in the Department of Social Sciences, Loughborough University. His chief areas of research lie in the areas of organization theory and research methodology. He has a special interest in leadership and organizational change and has undertaken a number of projects in this area. His most recent books as author or co-author are: *Quality and Quantity in Social Research* (Unwin Hyman, 1988), *Research Methods and Organization Studies* (Unwin Hyman, 1989), *Quantitative Data Analysis for Social Scientists* (Routledge, 1990), and *Charisma and Leadership in Organizations* (Sage, in press). He is editor of *Doing Research In Organizations* (Routledge, 1988).

Martyn Hammersley is Reader in Educational and Social Research, School of Education, The Open University. He has written extensively on research methodology. He is co-author of *Ethnography: Principles in Practice* (Tavistock, 1983), and author of *The Dilemma of Qualitative Method* (Routledge, 1989), *Reading Ethnographic Research* (Longman, 1991), *What's Wrong with Ethnography?* (Routledge, 1992).

Heather Laurie is Senior Research Officer with the British Household Panel Study, ESRC Research Centre, University of Essex. Her research interests include the internal dynamics of the household and women's labour market participation. She is currently writing her doctoral thesis.

Michael Little is Research Fellow at the Dartington Social Research Unit in the School of Applied Social Studies, University of Bristol. He has conducted research on young people in institutions and is the author of *Young Men in Prison* (Dartmouth, 1990).

Spencer Millham is Director of the Dartington Research Unit and Professor of Social Policy in the School of Applied Social Studies, University of Bristol. His many writings include co-authorship of *After Grace-Teeth* (Chaucer, 1975), *Locking Up Children* (Saxon House, 1978), and *Lost in Care* (Gower, 1989).

Hazel Qureshi carried out research concerning people with learning difficulties and challenging behaviour whilst employed as Research Fellow at Hester Adrian Research Centre, Manchester University. She has undertaken research on a wide range of topics in the field of formal and informal social care. She is a co-author of *The Caring Relationship* (Macmillan, 1989) and *Helpers in Case-Managed Community Care* (Gower, 1989). She is now Senior Researcher at the National Institute for Social Work.

Acknowledgements

Barbara Tizard and Carolyn Davies set me on course to edit this book. I am very grateful to them for their ideas and support. Recognition must also go to the Department of Health who commissioned me to write a paper on combining qualitative and quantitative methods and who also funded me to organize a training seminar on the subject at the Institute of Education in June 1989. For these are the origins of the book. Thanks are also due to the many researchers who discussed the issue with me, Jane Ritchie and Alan Bryman in particular, and also to all those who contributed papers to or took part in the seminar.

The production of the book has been somewhat of a tour de force because of the publisher's requirement for camera-ready copy. I would like to thank Mary Ward for all her help and enthusiasm in undertaking the formidable task of turning the manuscript into a book. I would like to take the opportunity also to thank others who have helped in various ways. They include Maria Harrison for help with the typing, Alex Brannen for the copy editing and Mary Douglas for useful advice. Lastly, mention must be made of the contributors who have been a pleasure to work with and without whom there would be no book.

Introduction

Julia Brannen

This edited volume has a history. It grew out of a series of interesting discussions held some two years ago between Carolyn Davies (Department of Health), Barbara Tizard (former Director of the Thomas Coram Research Unit), Jane Ritchie (Head of Qualitative Research at SCPR), and myself concerning the need for research training. We all agreed that the issue of combining quantitative and qualitative approaches was an important one which would be of considerable interest to old hands as well as new researchers.

In 1989 the Department of Health awarded me a grant to write a paper overviewing the issue (upon which Chapter 1 is based), and to organize a training seminar for researchers, including those employed in Department of Health funded research units. The seminar, held at the Institute of Education in June 1989, was deemed to be a great success. Its aim was to cover the larger theoretical and methodological questions that arise in mixing methods while also presenting the realpolitik and practical side of the research process. The sessions were therefore a mix of case studies of research projects which combined quantitative and qualitative methods together with presentations covering the more general questions raised by this research strategy.

In order to ensure that the issues discussed reached a wider audience it was proposed that there should be an edited book based on the seminar. As editor I have been fortunate in that important contributors to the seminar were also able to write chapters for the book. The --

methodological expertise of Martyn Hammersley and Alan Bryman has been invaluable in both types of contribution.

The reasons for the interest in the issue of multiple methods are several. One is the fact that there is relatively little space given to the issue in methodology textbooks. Another is that there are few studies employing both quantitative and qualitative methods which have explicitly discussed the methodological implications of the strategy. With the notable exception of Bryman's work (Bryman, 1988), there have been virtually no whole books devoted to the issue since, almost twenty years ago, Sieber wrote the following:

> The adjustments in traditional research designs called for by the integration of field and survey methods would seem to produce a new style of research. At present there are too few examples of this style to adduce general principles to be followed in organizing future projects. The task of collecting specimens of projects that have sought to benefit from the interplay of fieldwork and surveys, rather than instances bearing on a single aspect of projects, remains for the methodologist of the future - providing that the boundaries between the two traditions are dissolved and attention is turned to their intellectual integration in the interest of improving our strategies in social research (Sieber, 1973, p.1358).

A third reason for the current interest is to do with fashion among funders. Especially in social policy arenas, there is a growing interest in qualitative data (Walker, 1989), an interest which is set within the overall context of a long history of respect for quantitative, statistical data (Finch, 1986). A fourth factor has to do with current developments within the social sciences. Particularly in sociology, the 1980s brought not only a renewed growth in empirical research but also the harsh economic climate of the period injected a new realism whereby it was necessary to make the most of whatever research methods were strategic. In lean times it is expedient to overcome to some extent purist and sectarian tendencies, whether they are to do with discipline, theoretical perspectives or methods.

The structure and content of the book

The book is in two parts. Part One covers general considerations in employing a multiple method strategy (Chapters 1, 2 and 3). Part Two includes contributions from researchers who have adopted a combined approach in their particular studies (Chapters 4, 5, 6 and 7).

It is important to stress that the studies discussed in Part Two which employed multiple methods did not set out as models of this approach. Indeed for the most part the researchers' reflections on the topic have been prompted by the occasion of writing for this book. As editor, I am therefore extremely grateful for their courage and honesty in exposing their research practices and reflections thereon to the public gaze. It has long been the tendency, and still remains so in many circles, to represent one's methodological practice as if it exactly matched the textbook paradigm. It is to be hoped that others will learn and benefit from these accounts of research experience.

In Chapter 1, I present an overview of the issue. The chapter lays out the ways in which qualitative and quantitative research paradigms are said to differ and the ways in which they also overlap. It goes on to outline the different ways in which a combined approach can be employed and next considers some of the theoretical implications of this research strategy. Proclaiming the importance of choosing one's research methods in relation to the ways in which research problems are formulated and conceptualised, the view is taken that it is important to treat the data sets produced by each method as complementary to one another rather than to integrate them unproblematically. This proposition is tempered by a consideration of the effects of the research context upon choice of method: the established preferences of policy makers, the predilections of research funders, the constraints of discipline boundaries and political perspectives, the nature of the research career and the social organization of the research team. The chapter concludes with a discussion of the main ways qualitative and quantitative approaches are combined in research projects; attention is paid to the structure of the research process.

In Chapter 2, Martyn Hammersley attacks a purist, dichotomous position which suggests that qualitative and quantitative approaches can be clearly distinguished one from the other. A highly respected commentator upon qualitative and ethnographic methods (Hammersley and Atkinson 1983; Hammersley, 1989), he makes a number of important observations about the logic of scientific enquiry and clarifies common misunderstandings concerning inductive versus deductive processes and their association with particular types of method in the social sciences. His argument is that rather than being derived from philosophical or methodological commitments, choice of method should be based on the goals and circumstances of the research being pursued.

In Chapter 3, Alan Bryman adds new observations on the combination of qualitative and quantitative approaches to those already to be found (Bryman, 1988). He raises important issues about 'triangulation': how far different methods tap the same things; when findings derived from different data sets are inconsistent, the importance of pursuing the enquiry to find out why; the difficulty of deciding how far different data sets conflict and how far they simply qualify findings. More contentious is a discussion in which Bryman distinguishes between genuine and false ways of combining qualitative and quantitative research such as the quantification of essentially qualitative material, a situation in which the treatment of data is at variance with the type of method used.

The first case study of research presented in Part Two which uses multiple methods is the work of the Dartington Social Research Unit concerning children and families. In Chapter 4, Roger Bullock, Michael Little and Spencer Millham argue that a prior commitment to either qualitative or quantitative methods is rarely appropriate. Rather it is the theoretical perspective which ought to determine choice of method. Reviewing the body of research conducted in their unit, the authors note that none of their studies has exclusively adopted one approach at the expense of the other. Their strategy has been to apply middle range theories to their research problems, a process which has led to research designs which incorporate both quantitative and qualitative methods. The fact that a group of social policy researchers takes such a methodologically principled position is interesting given that social policy research, in contrast to other types of research, is widely regarded as particularly subject to external constraints. (See, for example, Chapters 1 and 3.)

Chapter 5 is also a case study of social policy research. However Hazel Qureshi takes a rather different position from the authors of Chapter 4 in that her concerns have less to do with theory and more to do with policy and the practicalities of research. Her choice of both qualitative and quantitative methods was the result of factors both intrinsic and extrinsic to her research. On the one hand, service agencies had a requirement for particular kinds of (statistical) data while, on the other, an appropriate method was needed for the study of a sensitive issue, namely asking parents about the behaviour problems of their mentally handicapped children. She used qualitative research to great effect to generate different kinds of data which are treated (with the use of a computer) both qualitatively and quantitatively in the analysis, a practice which is also referred to in Chapters 1 and 3.

Chapter 6 takes up the issue discussed by Martyn Hammersley in Chapter 2 - the argument that there is no necessary correspondence between particular methods and types of logical inference. In this chapter Margaret Bird describes a piece of research, also with a policy angle, which employs a case study design in order to illuminate theory - to discover and to test which factors are critical to the success of the Open College policy. Margaret Bird's choice of research design, the case study, itself demanded a combination of methods. In this chapter, she describes in detail the logic of enquiry which structures the research process. Her account charts the ways in which different methods and their corresponding data sets, drawn from both sides of the qualitative/quantitative divide, are used both inductively and deductively in a continuous interactive process of testing and reformulating hypotheses. Her account also draws attention to the practical exigencies upon choice of methods and their implementation, especially the role of the researcher as insider.

The final chapter describes a complex research situation: a project which aimed to generate data in its own right but was also designed to develop questions to be incorporated in a questionnaire for a large scale panel survey (the British Household Panel Study). In this account Heather Laurie suggests that the 'logical separation' between methods is less important in practice than is commonly assumed. In developing a qualitative project designed to explore financial arrangements in multi-adult and three generation households, the study drew upon Pahl's typology of household financial management systems (Pahl, 1989). Interestingly Heather Laurie reports that the qualitative approach did not necessarily lead to greater clarification of all the issues. Moreover she also concludes that the task of transposing questions to be put to research participants from one side of the quantitative/qualitative divide to the other is less problematic than might be supposed. The main problems which arose in this research concerned time and space considerations in the design of the questionnaire.

References

Bryman, A. (1988) *Quantity and Quality in Social Research.* London: Unwin Hyman.

Finch, J. (1986) *Research and Policy: The uses of qualitative methods in social and educational research.* Lewes: Falmer Press.

Hammersley, M. and Atkinson, P. (1983) *Ethnography: Principles in Practice.* London: Tavistock.

Hammersley, M. (1989) *The Dilemma of Qualitative Method: Herbert Blumer and the Chicago Tradition.* London: Routledge and Kegan Paul.

Pahl, J. (1989) *Money and Marriage.* London: Macmillan.

Sieber, S.D. (1973) 'The integration of fieldwork and survey methods'. *American Journal of Sociology, 78*, 6, pp.1335-1359.

Walker, R. (1989) 'We would like to know why: Qualitative research and the policy maker'. *Research Policy and Planning, 7*, 2, pp.15-21.

Part I

Considerations using multi-methods

1 Combining qualitative and quantitative approaches: an overview

Julia Brannen

Introduction

Traditionally a gulf is seen to exist between qualitative and quantitative research, with each belonging to distinctively different paradigms (Layder, 1988). The distinctions between the paradigms relate to a number of levels concerning the production of knowledge and the research process: the rarefied level of epistemology, the level of 'middle range' theory as elucidated in the theoretical framework, and the level of methods and techniques. There is assumed to be a correspondence between epistemology, theory and method. However the distinction is most commonly applied at the level of method: the process of data collection and the form in which the data are recorded and analyzed. Although many researchers see themselves as belonging to one or other paradigm, others happily combine methods.

The combining of different methods within a single piece of research raises the question of movement between paradigms at the levels of epistemology and theory. Whether or not such movement occurs, the process of combining methods highlights the importance of choosing the appropriate methods for the research questions and theory. Of course, as all researchers soon come to realise, the practice of research is a messy and untidy business which rarely conforms to the models set down in methodology textbooks. In practice it is unusual, for example, for epistemology or theory to be the sole determinant of method. The cart often comes before the horse, with the researcher already committed to a particular method before he or she has taken due time to consider the repertoire of methods suited to exploring the particular research issues. Researchers are often required to conduct balancing acts between a number of pragmatic considerations, responding at one and the same time to a number of constituencies - disciplinary, organizational and those related to the funding context.

The chapter will consider some of the issues and problems in combining methods in social science research. As a preliminary, the first section will consider the main distinctions according to which qualitative and quantitative paradigms are said to differ. The second section will briefly examine the methodology of combining methods, while the third section will consider some of the justifications for and implications of doing so, the most important being to do with theory. I will then turn, in the fourth section, to some of the major practical constraints which force researchers to adopt one method rather than another - the funding context, the academic setting, the organization of the research team and political considerations. The final section will consider the different ways in which qualitative and quantitative approaches can be and are combined in empirical studies.

Qualitative and quantitative paradigms

Most methodological commentaries seem to agree that, in so far as two distinct paradigms can be said to exist, the most important difference is the way in which each tradition treats data. In theory, if not in practice, the quantitative researcher isolates and defines variables and variable categories. These variable are linked together to frame hypotheses often before the data are collected, and are then tested upon the data. In contrast, the qualitative researcher begins with defining very general concepts which, as the research progresses, change their definition. For the former, variables are the vehicles or means of the analysis while, for the latter, they may constitute the product or outcome. The qualitative researcher is said to look through a wide lens, searching for patterns of inter-relationships between a previously unspecified set of concepts, while the quantitative researcher looks through a narrow lens at a specified set of variables.

A second important difference is said to turn on data collection. In the qualitative tradition, researchers must use themselves as the instrument, attending to their own cultural assumptions as well as to the data. In seeking to achieve imaginative insights into the respondents' social worlds the investigator is expected to be flexible and reflexive and yet somehow manufacture distance (McCracken, 1988). The consequence of this approach is that the method of qualitative research par excellence is participant observation. In the quantitative tradition, the instrument is a pre-determined and finely-tuned technological tool which allows for much less flexibility, imaginative input and reflexivity. For example, where the research issue is clearly defined and the questions put to respondents require unambiguous answers, a quantitative method such as a questionnaire may be appropriate. By contrast, where the research issue is less clear-cut and the questions to respondents likely to result in complex, discursive replies, qualitative techniques such as in-depth interviewing may be called for. A third difference, which I will discuss in more detail below, concerns the question of extrapolation and generalizability.

The differences which researchers feel exist between qualitative and quantitative approaches (whether or not these distinctions are logical ones) have profound effects on the focus and conduct of research projects, especially the choice of method. Many researchers do not regard different methods as substitutable for one another since they associate them with very different theoretical perspectives and different conceptualizations of research problems, whereby different realities or different aspects of reality are observed and captured. Decisions about methods also have implications for the training and skills of researchers and for the resourcing and social organization of projects.

In the following sub-sections I shall discuss in more detail some of the ways in which qualitative and quantitative paradigms overlap and differ in logical terms. Most importantly, to what extent are they informed by the same or different logics of enquiry?

Analytic induction versus enumerative induction

Quantitative research is typically associated with the process of enumerative induction. One of its main purposes is to discover how many and what kinds of people in the general or parent population have a particular characteristic which has been found to exist in the sample population. The aim is to infer a characteristic or a relationship between variables to a parent population. With qualitative research it is the concepts and categories, not their incidence and frequency, that are said to matter. 'In other words qualitative work does not survey the terrain, it mines it' (McCracken, 1988, p.17). Moreover, in so far as qualitative work is theoretical in its aims rather than descriptive - this is especially so with case studies that use qualitative methods - it is the testing of theory that is important rather than the issue of inference or generalizability (Yin, 1989; Platt, 1988).

While quantitative methods have been associated with enumerative induction, qualitative methods have been typically associated with analytic induction. The term analytic induction, as understood by its original exponents Znaniecki (1934) and Lindesmith (1938), was defined in contra-distinction to enumerative induction, as described above. However, contrary to current common sense beliefs about science, in the view of Znaniecki and Lindesmith, the main methods of the natural sciences (which are assumed to be in the quantitative paradigm) are not synonymous with inferential statistics; rather they involve the process of analytic induction. In analytic induction the researcher moves from the data through the formulation of hypotheses to their testing and verification.

Because enumerative induction is sometimes seen to be wrongly associated with the natural sciences, analytic induction as applied in qualitative research has sometimes attracted the criticism of being 'unscientific'. Moreover, it is not always well understood that analytic induction, as used by Lindesmith for example, may combine an inductive logic of enquiry (which begins with an absence of clear hypotheses) with deductive methods, namely the testing of hypotheses (Hammersley, 1985; 1989). It also needs saying here that a lot of qualitative research is simply descriptive.

Analytic induction is most frequently employed in ethnographic work (Hammersley and Atkinson, 1983; Silverman, 1985). The process begins with the 'immersion' of the researcher in the field. At the start the research problem is only roughly defined. A concrete case is inspected and those features which are essential to it are abstracted (Znaniecki, 1934; Denzin, 1970). A working hypothetical explanation of the phenomenon, as roughly identified in the case, is then formulated; the determination as to whether the facts fit the explanation is carried out on a case by case basis. If a case does not fit the facts, either the explanation is reformulated or the phenomenon redefined so that the deviant or negative case is excluded. The explanation is deemed to have been confirmed after a succession of cases have been examined and the hypothesis found to fit the evidence in each successive case. The procedure continues to the point of saturation when no more negative cases are found. (See Berthaux, 1981.) For some exponents of analytic induction, notably Lindesmith, the process continues until a universal relationship or law is established, each case raising the possibility of redefinition or reformulation which, as described above, the researcher may then go on to test. In this last respect Lindesmith's study of opiate addiction is a striking and rare example of the approach in action (Lindesmith, 1968).

Enumerative and analytic induction have different starting points therefore: enumerative induction abstracts by generalizing whereas analytic induction generalizes by abstracting.

> The former looks in many cases for characters that are similar and abstracts them conceptually because of their generality, presuming that they must be essential to each particular case; the latter abstracts from the given concrete case characters that are essential to it and generalises them, presuming that in so far as they are essential, they are similar in many cases (Znaniecki, 1934, pp.250-1).

Many features of analytic induction are shared by grounded theory, as first formulated by Glaser and Strauss (1967). Grounded theory holds a central place in the qualitative paradigm. However there are important differences as well as similarities. The main difference is that analytic induction is concerned with developing and testing relatively simple explanatory hypotheses, whereas the latter is concerned with developing rather complex theories. Secondly, grounded theory differs from analytic induction in its adoption of a constant comparative method, involving the comparison of multiple data segments judged to belong to the same category, in such a way as to identify the central features of that category. As the analysis develops, the categories become the central organizers of the material (Hammersley, 1989, p.175). A third difference is the issue of theoretical sampling whereby cases or groups are strategically selected in order to maximize theoretical differences or similarities. The researcher may begin by minimizing the differences between comparison groups in order to bring out the basic properties of a category. Only when this has been done will the researcher employ the strategy of maximizing differences (Hammersley, 1989, p.176).

In the practice of social science research these differences between the two types of induction are less marked than they appear in theory. As Hammersley argues in Chapter 2, it is common and over-simplistic for researchers using qualitative methods to contrast their own inductive reasoning with deductive logic. Quantitative research does not always test hypotheses: its goal is often descriptive. As Bulmer (1979) has noted with respect to grounded theory, although the rules are such that they initially demand the suspension of awareness of relevant categories and concepts, there are grounds for scepticism. Qualitative researchers do have ideas about what they expect to find or intend to look for, albeit not necessarily ideas to which they are heavily committed before the data collection phase begins. Even if researchers lack a clear set of hypotheses at the start of their researches their ideas cannot help but be influenced by their prior knowledge of the literature and by their repertoires of lay knowledge, including political values and previous research and common sense experience. Qualitative work is to some extent always theory driven, though it is often criticised for being atheoretical. The charge is frequently levied that qualitative researchers are reluctant to inject theory into their interpretation of the data by sticking too closely to respondents' constructs and interpretative devices (Rock, 1973; Delamont, 1981; Hammersley, 1985).

Criticism of quantitative work which turns on its positivistic assumptions makes similar accusations however - charging it with being atheoretical and data driven. The fact that both are subject to similar criticisms is perhaps not so paradoxical when we consider the extent to which there is overlap in their respective logics of enquiry.

Generalization versus extrapolation

Part of the issue concerning the logic of enquiry is, according to the quantitative paradigm, to do with generalizability: how far the findings can be generalized to a general or parent population. In selecting a sample, care needs to be taken so that no bias is introduced into the sample; within a specified range of certainty, which is precisely estimated (using probability theory), characteristics of the parent population are accurately reflected. Where statistical inferences are made concerning the linking of two characteristics in the parent population the inference is only about concomitant variation of the two characteristics. However, if the quantitative researcher is interested in causal explanations it is also necessary to go beyond statistical correlation and issues of representativeness and to resort to theoretical thinking about the linkages between the two characteristics (Mitchell, 1983).

In qualitative research, which is not based upon statistical samples, the issue of generalisability does not arise in the same way. The questions are rather different ones. The concern is about the replication of the findings in other similar cases or sets of conditions. In the instance of case studies for example, the issue needs to be couched in terms of how far the findings can be extrapolated to the theory that the research has been designed to test. Inferences are usually theoretical or causal unless of course cases are selected according to probability sampling. Issues about the representativeness of the sample and the generalizability of the findings are not salient; rather it is the issue of establishing a theoretical link within each case.

In practice those working with quantitative methods frequently elide theoretical and statistical inference. Accordingly, when an association is found between variables in a statistical sample, theoretical connections are postulated rather than established. A theoretical connection is also presumed to exist in a parent population simply because the features can be inferred to co exist in that population (Mitchell, 1983).

Issues of generalizability and extrapolation are closely tied to the process of selecting cases for study. Where heavily quantitative methods are used, in surveys for example, samples are random or representative since there is a need to generalize. In so far as qualitative methods are employed on non statistical samples, 'sampling' may be conducted on the basis of theoretical criteria. The basic question in theoretical sampling is which case or group to turn to next in the analysis and with what theoretical purpose. Unlike the quantitative researcher, the qualitative researcher is expected to redefine the criteria governing the choice of comparison groups as the analysis proceeds on a case by case basis. The selection of cases cannot therefore be planned in advance, as is the case with investigations which use predominantly statistical methods. For example, Glaser and Strauss selected comparison groups for their study of patients who were dying in hospital on the following basis. Since, in the course of their immersion in the field, they had become sensitized to the different kinds of awareness contexts with respect to death, they selected different types of hospital wards according to the imminence or likelihood with which hospital staff expected death to occur; thus intensive care wards were contrasted with cancer wards and with premature baby units. Glaser and Strauss also imaginatively contrasted hospital awareness contexts with other types of awareness context, for example situations in which black people 'pass' as white (Glaser and Strauss, 1967).

In theoretical sampling, there is a further question as to the number of cases or groups to choose. There are no definitive guidelines here. A balance needs to be struck between the point of theoretical saturation and the availability of time and money. By contrast statistical sampling is, as I have already noted, linked to the question of statistical inference - the question of whether the sample, within certain limits of probability, is thought to reflect the parent population. Within the quantitative paradigm, questions need also to be settled about comparison groups. The decisions here are usually less to do with the central theoretical question of the research and more often to do with the expected (often structural) variations in the general population which the researchers want to control for in the testing of hypotheses. For example, social attitude surveys conducted in the quantitative paradigm routinely do breakdowns by social class, sex and age. In their more extreme form the primary aim of such surveys is not to theorize about the nature of the relationship between attitudes and demographic factors but to infer the associations found to the parent population.

Statistical and theoretical sampling strategies can be used in combination in order to identify representative and unrepresentative cases. Surveys will readily identify the main representative types of case while a theoretical sampling strategy facilitates the identification of cases that do and do not conform to theoretical expectations (Sieber, 1973). In the latter case the process has come to be known as deviant case analysis.

> Through careful analysis of the cases which do not exhibit the expected behaviour the researcher recognizes the over-simplification of his theoretical structure and becomes aware of the need for incorporating further variables into his predictive scheme (Kendall and Wolf, 1949, pp.153-4).

There is therefore no necessary link between choice of method and logic of enquiry, type of inference and sampling strategy. Qualitative methods such as in-depth interviews can draw upon a statistical logic of enquiry, though they tend not to. Questionnaires and structured interview techniques may be used to good effect in exploring theory.

The methodology of combining approaches

The existence of two distinct paradigms suggests something about researchers' allegiances if not their practices. This is not surprising since the body of methodology texts which attests to the existence of the two paradigms is much larger than the body of literature which instructs researchers in the conduct of multi-method research. It is to the latter that I now turn.

Burgess chooses the term 'multiple research strategies' to describe the use of diverse methods in tackling a research problem (Burgess, 1982). According to this view, field methods which do not encompass observation, informant interviewing and sampling are seen as narrow and inadequate. The argument is that researchers ought to be flexible and therefore ought to select a range of methods that are appropriate to the research problem under investigation (Burgess, 1984).

The older and more widely used terminology to be found in the literature which refers to this strategy is 'triangulation', a term which was originally borrowed from psychological reports (see Campbell and Fiske, 1959) and developed by Denzin (1970). For Denzin, triangulation does not merely involve methods and data but investigators and theories as well (Denzin, 1970, p.310). By and large researchers have taken the term to mean more than one method of investigation and hence more than one type of data (Bryman, 1988, p.131). Drawing on Denzin, I will now outline different types of triangulation.

Multiple methods Method triangulation may be between-methods or within-method. A within-method approach involves the same method being used on different occasions, while between-methods means using different methods in relation to the same object of study, substantive issue etc. Thus in the latter case participant observation in a classroom setting may be combined with a questionnaire survey of pupils and teachers. A within-method approach may involve repeating the same method on a number of occasions and may produce different assessments of the situation at different times. Observers in the field do something similar when, at a later point in time, they consider their field notes and come to a fresh consideration of their observations.

Multiple investigators Here research is carried out by partnerships or teams rather than by one individual. Research organization is an important part of research strategy: different individuals and different mixes of individuals bring different perspectives to the research depending upon the disciplines they belong to, their theoretical and political persuasions, their gender, age and social backgrounds. Even if each researcher uses the same research method he or she is likely to bring a different viewpoint to the research which may influence the way he or she views the data. For example, Stacey (1960), commenting on her first study of Banbury, indicates that the three researchers who comprised the research team reflected the three different social classes - class being a key focus of the Banbury study - the titled upper, the lower middle, and the working class.

Multiple data sets   Different data sets may be derived through the application of different methods, but also through the use of the same method at different times or with different sources. Data may be collected from a range of family members rather than one individual family member reporting upon the actions and activities of others. Data may be collected at different points in time and in a variety of contexts, situations and settings. Furthermore, data may relate to different levels of social analysis: the individual level, the interactive or the collective level.

An example of multiple data sets is taken from my own research experience, namely a study of dual earner households in early parenthood. The project employed psychologists, sociologists and social policy researchers using a variety of methods, a longitudinal design (four time points) and a range of sources - mothers, children and the children's carers. The data gathered included: scores from child development tests, observations concerning mother child relationships, information from diaries kept by the mothers, responses from structured and semi-structured interviews conducted with the mothers (Brannen and Moss, 1991).

Multiple theories   As well as multiple data sets researchers may employ multiple theories. Initial data analysis, together with insights from the research process itself, may generate a number of possible theories and hypotheses about the research problem in question. These may in turn be tested out on the data. Alternatively, an examination of prior research may lead the researcher to test a number of plausible and possibly competing hypotheses on his or her findings. Psychological studies which test low level theories provide plenty of examples here.

Theoretical implications of combining approaches - integration versus complementarity

There is much controversy as to the conditions under which multiple methods ought to be combined. Some researchers have talked in terms of the complementarity of the two approaches. By this is meant that each approach is used in relation to a different research problem or different aspect of a research problem. By contrast Denzin, in his original formulation of triangulation, saw the combining of research strategies as a means of examining the same research problem and hence of enhancing claims concerning the validity of the conclusions that could be reached about the data (Denzin, 1970). In Denzin's view, the assumption was that the data generated by the two approaches, which were assumed to focus on the same research problem, were consistent with and were to be integrated with one another. By contrast in the first view, the different data sets were not expected to be consistent; rather they were seen to be complementary.

In line with the first view it has been frequently noted that the assumption that combining approaches ensures the validity of data is naive (Fielding and Fielding, 1986, p.31; Hammersley and Atkinson, 1983, p.199; Bryman, 1988, p.133). Indeed the differences between different data sets are likely to be as illuminating as their points of similarity. The idea that data generated by different methods can simply be aggregated to produce a single unitary picture of what is assumed to be the 'truth' (i.e. valid) is often encountered among positivists. Rather data can only be understood in relation to the purposes for which they are created, for example the production or testing of theory. If the purposes differ, the data sets cannot be integrated.

The differences between the two positions outlined above - the 'integrationists' and those who see integration as problematic - are at the heart of what some regard as an epistemological divide underpinning many of the distinctions between qualitative and quantitative approaches. Tensions arise with respect to differing types of explanation and the nature of data itself.

In some cases whole substantive areas may be riven by different methodologies which do not lead to an easy integration of the findings. For example, in a review of research concerning recent major geographical shifts in the British economy, Massey and Allen contrast two types of studies: large scale, cross-sectional data sets which focus on vast industrial swathes of the economy and those focusing on a small number of cases in a particular industry (Massey and Allen, 1988). The drift of this debate is that the two types of studies produce two types of competing explanations. While the first school of thought is said to focus on short term 'outcomes' across the whole economy, the second school looks at longer term 'processes' of change within particular industries and sectors of industry. (The distinction between outcomes and processes is important and the language redolent of underlying theoretical persuasions.) The first school addresses itself to a general theory of causation across the whole economy, while the second school provides evidence that similar outcomes result from different causes. The authors in question are somewhat rejecting of the first school and conclude that it is futile to look for regular patterns across the whole economy (at least at this point in time). The argument about the incompatibility between the two types of study is about more than method alone and relates also to underlying, unstated assumptions about theory and epistemology.

Research projects are influenced, though not necessarily completely determined, as I shall argue later, by theoretical assumptions about the nature of data and ideas about the constitution of the social world. While it is simplistic to divide the population of researchers on epistemological grounds into positivists and interpretativists (see Halfpenny (1979) for a discussion of this dichotomy), the distinction is a useful one in understanding data in terms of knowledge. Moreover, the distinction may not always be obvious to researchers despite their epistemological allegiances as they become absorbed in the nitty-gritty practicalities of devising a research project. In so far as data are treated as objective phenomena which unproblematically reflect the 'real' world, researchers will tend to pile up research findings in an additive way. Triangulation when it is used according to this formulation is simply eclecticism. If, on the other hand, data are considered in close relation to the questions and theories which generate them, researchers will adopt the method most appropriate to these. In this case data sets cannot simply be linked together unproblematically but need to be treated as complementary.

As Cain and Finch (1981) cogently argue, there is no one truth; life is merely multi-faceted. According to their view, the discovery of what 'really' happens is not the task of sociological investigation. At the extremes, advocates of the integration of methods assume that triangulation offers the opportunity to increase the 'internal validity' of the data. In contrast, those who favour complementarity recognize that data are constituted by the method which elicits them and that different data sets do not add up to some rounded unity.

Among those who use statistical methods these issues are addressed through the notion of validity. The conventional formulation of the problem is that data are somehow 'more valid' if they are generated by more than one type of instrument or more than one type of interview question. Rather, researchers who use qualitative methods question the nature of the data which constitute evidence. They are concerned with the ways in which data have been created: are they the product of the negotiation between interviewer and interviewee or are they actions or justifications of action given to other actors in a particular situation? They question the ways in which the data relate to the initial theories and initial formulations of the research problem (Cain and Finch, 1981, p.111).

Despite the dictat in methodology texts to match method to the conceptualisation of the research problem, there is the empirical question as to how far epistemological issues in practice determine methods. This question has been extensively explored by Bryman (1984; 1988). The converse question may also be posed, namely whether the use of a particular method inevitably means that a particular epistemological position has been adopted. Within the methodology literature which tells researchers how research ought to be done, epistemology and method are depicted as intimately inter-related. Quantitative methods are seen as having some kind of one-to-one correspondence with positivist epistemology, while qualitative methods are associated with an interpretative epistemology directed towards the uncovering of meaning (Halfpenny, 1979). Bryman has persuasively argued that, while this 'bracketing together' may be advocated in the methodology literature and constitutes good advice to researchers, in practice researchers select their methods on the basis of a variety of technical considerations (Bryman, 1984; 1988).

> There seems, then, to be a tendency for many writers to shuttle uneasily back and forth between epistemological and technical levels of discourse. While much of the exposition of the epistemological debates of qualitative research helped to afford it some credibility, a great many decisions about whether and when to use qualitative methods seems to have little, if any, recourse to these broader intellectual issues (Bryman, 1988, p.108).

While it is arguable that many of the considerations which researchers take account of in justifying their choice of methods are not obviously or solely theoretical, I would also add that, implicit in some technical decisions, are particular ways of conceptualising research problems which relate, if only indirectly, to larger epistemological questions. Undoubtedly, as Bryman argues and others have demonstrated (see for example Platt (1986) who shows the lack of fit between a functionalist perspective and survey methods), there is no necessary or one-to-one correspondence between epistemology and methods. However, this is not to gainsay that the matching of methods to research problems, rather than research problems to methods, is what every researcher should aim for.

A further theoretical justification for combining qualitative and quantitative approaches is as a strategy which provides a solution to what sociological theorists term 'the duality of structure' (Giddens, 1976). I refer here to the macro-structural ways of understanding society, which tend to call forth a deterministic explanatory mode, versus those micro-structural approaches which emphasize creative and interactive explanations and processes. According to Cicourel (1981), it is not possible to 'dissolve' the micro/macro dimension, as the rationale underlying Denzin's exposition of triangulation implies. Rather these two different theoretical frameworks are to be seen as different levels of enquiry which cannot be addréssed through the same method.

Against the argument that structure can be theorised at both macro- and micro-levels, some qualitative researchers argue that concrete social interactions constitute the basis of both levels of social structure, that in effect macro-phenomena are unknown and unknowable. (See Fielding, 1988.) A way out of this situation is offered by 'methodological situationalism' whereby macro-level phenomena, such as social class, must be accounted for through the study of social relationships - namely interaction in social situations not individual behaviour (Knorr-Cetina, 1988; Fielding and Fielding, 1986; Fielding, 1988). In other words descriptively adequate accounts of large scale social phenomena should be grounded in statements about actual social behaviour in concrete situations (Fielding, 1988). In practice, however, much qualitative work makes explicit reference to institutional concepts which are not reducible to interactionist terms.

Even if researchers are unable to achieve such ambitious aims, at the very least their methods ought to be related to a particular level of enquiry and they should attempt to relate these different levels to one another. There may therefore be a good theoretical case for combining methods in order to study different levels of enquiry and in order to explore different aspects of the same problem. Through the careful and purposeful combination of different methods breadth and depth are added to the analysis (Fielding and Fielding, 1986).

At the very least the multi-method approach demands that the researcher specifies, as precisely as possible, the particular aims of each method, the nature of the data that is expected to result, and how the data relate to theory. In so far as findings which result from different methods are at odds or conflict with one another, these seeming contradictions ought to be addressed by the researchers in their interpretation of the data and in the linkages they make between methods, data and theory. Discrepancies should also prompt the researcher to probe particular issues in greater depth. In their own right, these may lead to new theories and more fruitful areas of enquiry.

Such care and precision are needed at all stages in the research process from the design stage to writing up. For example, since qualitative research designs often adopts a non probability sampling strategy (in contrast to quantitative work), it is important to be clear at the design stage why and when it is appropriate to have probability samples and the consequences of the resulting types of data which follow from such decisions. In writing up two data sets - one from a probability sample and another from a non probability one - the language of 'representativeness' needs to be handled carefully, as the text switches from one to the other.

probability v non - probability sampling

Practical constraints upon combining methods

As Bryman (1988) has argued, the practice of social research is also governed by constraints other than those of theory. The decision to combine (or not to combine) qualitative and quantitative methods is subject to a variety of considerations concerning the funding context and the available financial resources, the skills of researchers, the social organization and political orientations of the research team. This is not to say that these constraints are necessarily a bad thing in the sense that they divert the researcher from the 'correct' aims of the research such as the advancement of theory. Rather they are the unavoidable social context in which research is conducted.

The funding context - the case of social policy research

An important constraint upon choice of methods is the funding context - the requirements of the funders and the researchers' perceptions of the funders and also their perceptions of what the funders expect researchers to provide.

With respect to the field of social policy research, I will summarise Finch's extensive and well-argued case that some methods have been preferred to the exclusion of others (Finch, 1986). Accordingly, Finch argues that there is a long-established preference in government for the quantitative paradigm which goes back to the influence of Booth and Rowntree. This tradition requires that researchers provide 'facts', usually statistical ones, which are presumed to be quintessentially neutral in a political or value sense. Within this paradigm, the researcher is placed in the role of the technician and the decision as to which 'facts' are relevant and how they are to be interpreted and used are firmly in the hands of policy makers.

While government expectations as to what passes for policy-relevant research undoubtedly help to shape government funded research projects, it should be added that researchers may also collude in meeting such expectations by assuming that other (i.e. qualitative approaches) are unacceptable to policy makers. Yet whatever the locus of constraints, it is the case that in historical terms, social policy research in Britain has, until recently, largely eschewed qualitative approaches.

As Finch also argues, the reasons for the separation of qualitative research from social policy also lie in the separate development of the two disciplines of sociology and social administration. In the case of British sociology, there was a period in which the qualitative tradition began to come to the fore (the 1960s). This was also precisely the time at which sociologists were distancing themselves both from the empirical tradition and from social policy research. These traditions were seen as essentially technical and applied and hence as subject to political manipulation. This occurred with the re-emergence of the sociology of knowledge and the impact of European schools of thought, which led to a dramatic move within university departments of sociology away from empirically driven work and towards theory (Finch, 1986).

There are reasons for believing that the conditions under which the quantitative paradigm has been dominant in British sociological and policy relevant research are changing. The first relates to the economic climate, especially the stringent economic conditions in which research is funded today - large scale work is expensive for funders. The second relates to changes in the political culture which in turn have influenced the way in which the social sciences have been regarded in the 1980s in Britain and whether and in what ways they are used (Brannen, 1987). Given the existence of a radical and ideologically driven government during the 1980s, policy makers have had a lesser requirement for information in order to support and inform their decision making. Where political decisions are made primarily for ideological reasons the power of knowledge and experts is diminished and policies are created willy-nilly. The third reason relates to the diminishing autonomy of the universities and the requirement on them to be financially self-supporting and to make their own way in the market place, in the manner of private sector organizations, especially through marketing their wares. Universities are no longer able to justify their existence in terms of pursuing independent knowledge. This means that social researchers have had to respond to these changed times and to eschew purely theoretical research.

If it is the case that changes have taken place in the old dictats the time may be ripe for social policy researchers to break down the barriers between paradigms, especially by opting more for qualitative approaches. Changes in the political culture affect the context in which policy is made. This changing policy context in turn suggests that a diversity of strategies is required for feeding into the processes of policy making (Brannen, 1987). Where political processes become more significant and the bureaucracy of government less so (both central and local government) and if social science research is to be used, it needs to feed into all points of the political decision-making process and the different arenas of political influence. The judicious use of qualitative methods in conjunction with more traditional quantitative ones in the conduct of policy-relevant research may make a new and valuable contribution. (See Finch 1986, pp.157-74; and Chapters 4, 5, 6 and 7 for examples of such work.) Moreover limits upon funding provide an opportunity to move towards a highly strategic approach to the planning of research with the result that projects using different methods may be linked together, with each one building upon another.

At the more pragmatic, day-to-day level, funders have the power to promote or discourage particular kinds of studies. Since different methods require different amounts of resources - research skills, money and time - in times of financial stringency such constraints may dictate the kinds of projects for which researchers seek funding, as well as the size of research budgets and types of projects that funders are prepared to finance. It is often assumed, mistakenly, that qualitative approaches are cheaper than quantitative methods because fewer cases are studied. Projects which combine qualitative and quantitative methods are likely to be particularly costly, involving lengthy timetables and teams of researchers which have the range of relevant skills. Again a response to this challenge may be the development of linked studies which bridge a variety of methods.

Researchers: skills, careers and disciplines

The adoption of a multi-method approach is affected by the availability of appropriate talents in the academic setting and community. It is however rare for the individual researcher to be equally competent in both qualitative and quantitative methods. The typical research career rarely offers the opportunity to develop both sets of skills and, where it does, not to a balanced degree. Moreover, before the researcher embarks on a research career, any training he or she has acquired, for example through a course in research methods, will rarely have given equal weight to both qualitative and quantitative methods. In reality most researchers become practised in and identified with one set of skills since there is pressure to go on doing what one is good at and has done before. The 'trained incapacities' of researchers have been cited as a cause of the disinclination on the part of some researchers to combine methods, especially social survey methods with participant observation (Reiss, 1968, p.351).

Changing methods or adopting more than one method requires researchers to increase their repertoire of skills. There are many disincentives to change. A major constraint is that most research contracts are given on the assumption that training takes place on the job. It is therefore difficult to get training for something that one has not been hired to do. Moreover qualitative and quantitative methods require rather different talents for which individuals often have natural, as well as acquired, dispositions. Furthermore, the later in the research career the researcher leaves the acquisition of new skills the more difficult he or she is likely to find obtaining the time and resources necessary.

A related constraint against becoming a multi-talented researcher is the 'culture of impermanence' surrounding the research career (Bernstein, personal communication). The conditions of employment under which many researchers are employed are those of the short term contract, which provides limited opportunities for training and retraining. The researcher is forced to write a research proposal for a new research project in order to secure further employment while, at the same time, writing up the last piece of work. There is no legitimate time or space in which the researcher is able to consider, let alone retrain in, new approaches and new skills. Contract researchers are likely to experience unemployment between research contracts; unlike lecturing staff, they have no entitlement to sabbatical leave.

A further constraint concerns discipline boundaries and the association of particular disciplines with particular paradigms. Particular disciplines in the social sciences and particular traditions of thought are closely identified with quantitative methods; psychology, economics, and social policy are cases in point. By contrast the qualitative paradigm is to be found in social anthropology and particular branches of British sociology, with gender studies a striking example from the present and recent past.

The social organization of the research team

The lack of fit between theoretical issues and choice of methods in the practice of research was discussed earlier. An important factor which may inhibit the process whereby methods are chosen with respect to theory is the social organization of the research team, in particular situations where there is a sharply segregated division of labour (Kay, 1989). According to Kay (1989), this tends to occur where research is organized in terms of the model of the autonomous tenured academic (usually male) who is serviced by the contract research assistant (usually female). It is noteworthy that this time structuring of the research process is more common in quantitative than qualitative research.

In this model the academic, as chief investigator, has responsibility for the development of theory, which usually occurs at the stage of writing the proposal, and for the re-injection of theory at the final writing-up stage of the project. Typically, such a person plays little or no part in the fieldwork. Contrastingly, the hired hand researcher is usually not around for the development or writing-up of the project. She (hired hands are usually women) joins the team after the proposal and theoretical framework have been developed. Her job description largely requires her to perform a technical role - typically the fieldwork, data handling and the preliminary analysis. On her arrival she is put under pressure 'to display her skills' and is given little opportunity to reconsider the appropriateness of methods to the theoretical and conceptual demands of the project. That she has been selected because of specific skills is a further justification against further exploring questions of methodology in relation to theory. In short, this division of labour is not conducive to the production and maintenance of close links between theory, methods and analysis.

Political perspectives - the case of feminism

The final consideration governing the choice of methods concerns political values and perspectives (Bryman, 1988). A commitment to feminism is a case in point. To some extent the fact that qualitative methods have been preferred by many feminists is a reflection of the current or thus far historically-determined state of the art of methodology, since quantitative methods (as the dominant paradigm) have been exposed by some feminists as being associated with masculinist assumptions and bias. As Oakley (1981) and Graham (1983) have argued, the use of positivist approaches, namely surveys, have rendered women (and their perspectives) invisible. Surveys are not the objective, neutral and scientific instruments they claim to be but are imbued with masculinist assumptions. Yet although qualitative methods have been preferred by the majority of feminist researchers, the history of the use of such methods is less gender linked in terms of research personnel than one might expect (Finch, 1986, p.5). Moreover as Morgan (1981) also notes, there is an identifiable 'macho' style among certain strands of qualitative work which is especially discernible in the study of deviance and popular culture, both areas which have focused largely on men.

Yet there is no theoretical reason why a particular political perspective, namely feminism (and I use the term in a broad sense as there are many feminist theories), should be associated with only one type of research method. Indeed the explicit position of some feminists (Stanley and Wise, 1983) is that there is no one set of methods which should be seen as distinctly feminist; the more important issue is the investigation of sexism in society and the location of the researcher as feminist within the research process. Moreover there are grounds for arguing that both qualitative and quantitative approaches need to be applied in combination, especially where investigations are carried out on social groups whose material situations and perspectives have been under- or mis-represented in social research. While the qualitative approach may overcome some of the problems of giving a voice and language to such groups, through which they may better express their experiences, the quantitative approach would serve to indicate the extent and patterns of their inequality at particular historical junctures.

Political justifications for preferring qualitative over quantitative methods may also include ethical questions, namely the relation between the researcher and the researched, especially when the subjects of research comprise disadvantaged groups in society. It is argued by

Oakley (1981) in respect of studying women that the qualitative approach - the use of semi- or unstructured interviews - helps to mitigate some of the inequality which exists between the researcher and the researched and avoids further reinforcement of inequality among those who are already exploited. Others have since suggested that the issue is more complex (see for example, Finch, 1983). Indeed some have taken the view that it is the production of written texts rather than method per se which gives feminist researchers the power to represent the interests of women subjects (Stanley and Wise, 1983).

As has been suggested above, a feminist stance ought not necessarily to imply an allegiance to a particular methodology. The more important issue is the question of theory - in the case of women the theory of patriarchy - and the methods most appropriate for addressing it. It should therefore be possible to conduct statistical studies which test hypotheses guided by feminist theory as well as qualitative studies which enable women to speak for themselves.

Ways of combining multiple methods in the research process

Bryman (1988) has enumerated and explored three main ways in which those researchers who have drawn on both qualitative and quantitative methods in their work have combined them: qualitative work as a facilitator of quantitative work; quantitative work as a facilitator of qualitative work; both approaches are given equal emphasis. Drawing upon Bryman's classification, I propose to discuss in the final part of the paper some of the ways in which qualitative and quantitative approaches have been combined in the research process and with respect to particular examples of empirical research.

The process of combining approaches and methods is structured according to several factors. The first concerns the relative importance that is given to each approach within the overall project. The second concerns time ordering - the extent to which methods are carried out consecutively or simultaneously. It is obvious that the contribution of qualitative methods to the formulation of a theoretical problem which a survey then goes on to address requires that intensive fieldwork be performed prior to the survey. Furthermore, if the purpose of the qualitative fieldwork is to clarify or extend a survey finding, then it must be conducted after the survey. The third factor is also linked to time-ordering and concerns the stage in the research process at which the respective methods come into play or cease to be in evidence. For example, both methods may enter the project at the design stage but only one may figure in the writing-up of the project. The fourth factor governing their usage concerns the division of skills in the research team. In practice all these issues are inter-related though it may be useful to disentangle them as a means of illuminating the diverse ways in which different methods are combined in research projects.

In examining the accounts researchers give of their methodology it is of course not always possible to surmise what exactly took place, in what order, or the relative inputs of different methods and types of data. Publishers require that methodology sections of books are kept to a minimum. Journal articles are constrained by lack of space and rarely focus exclusively on the methodological aspects of research projects. Moreover there are informal pressures which come from the academic community in favour of concealment, for example the peer review process. Too often this process results in the researcher putting the 'best face' on his or her research so that methodological limitations are glossed over. In addition there are the constraints of the printed word whereby the researcher is required to give an authoritative account of his or her work (Clifford, 1986). These may mean displaying some methods and not others, notably those presumed to have greater credibility and legitimacy.

The following discussion is organized around the degree of pre-eminence given to qualitative and quantitative methods. In each sub-section I will consider the relationship between the two approaches in terms of time scheduling, the stage in the research process when they are introduced (or discounted), and the skills of the researchers.

The pre-eminence of the quantitative over the qualitative

Where qualitative methods play a subsidiary role in a project they are likely to have particular kinds of functions. First, they may act as a source of hunches or hypotheses which quantitative work may then go on to test. A second usage is in the development and piloting of research instruments - questionnaires, scales and indices. A third and often covert usage is in the interpretation and clarification of quantitative data. Here the quantitative researcher may draw on but not necessarily acknowledge qualitative material when he or she 'speculates' about the nature of the relationships which have been found to be statistically significant. Perhaps their most common usage is as exemplars of quantitative findings, especially in the fleshing out of variable categories.

Where qualitative methods are only marginally important there is likely to be a segregation of research skills on the project team. In general, since quantitative researchers rarely have much experience in qualitative methods, these skills often have to be imported from outside. Typically qualitative work is carried out prior to the main quantitative study. In general it seems to be a more frequent occurrence for qualitative researchers to use quantitative methods than it is for quantitative researchers to carry out qualitative approaches.

A current example of a qualitative researcher turning her hand to quantitative research is provided by Oakley who was previously rooted in the qualitative tradition. The project was a large scale quantitative investigation of the effects of social support on low birth weight (Oakley and Rajan, 1991). However since the research was also concerned with the evaluation of support and an exploration of the nature of support it included a qualitative component.

Qualitative work which plays a subsidiary role is more often than not a precursor to the quantitative work. It may take place at an early stage in the research process during the development of the instruments for data collection. In the case of social surveys, for example, qualitative methods may be used to some limited extent in the preparatory work, typically in the piloting of questionnaires - the trying out of questions and the development of codes with which to categorise responses. They may be similarly used to determine threshhold points on a rating scale.

The following example is a study where qualitative methods were employed in the early stages of the research process. It concerns a large prospective study in the quantitative mode which aimed to predict cases of depression among working-class women (Brown, 1988). The qualitative work occurred predominantly in the development of the research, and in the data collection phase. These stages were carried out largely by researchers trained in qualitative methods most of whom had left the project by the time the main analysis was carried out. One researcher was hired explicitly for the task of the developmental work - the identification of key concepts and their operationalisation within a quantitative paradigm. In the main study which followed, the research team was required to conduct in-depth interviews using a semi-structured schedule, having been given a thorough grounding in the concepts and their empirical measures. They were then required to sort the verbatim comments from the tape-recorded interviews according to the appropriate conceptual categories that had been devised and to transcribe the relevant comments under each. Drawing upon an agreed set of threshold examples, which were developed in the early exploratory study, each respondent was rated on each conceptual category on a four point scale. This detailed, time-consuming exercise required the interviewers to maintain close touch with the raw qualitative data in the preliminary stage of analysis. Once the data were quantified however there was little further role for the data in their qualitative verbatim form, neither in the analysis nor in the published findings.

In the above study of women's depression there was a presumption that qualitative approaches are technically useful i.e. in the generation of data through the use of in-depth interviewing. However these data were not considered to have a status in their own right. In so far as they contained meaning they were subject to quantification. Women's accounts of the significance they attributed to various aspects of their lives (deemed to be important to women's self-esteem and therefore important in the genesis of depression in times of adversity) were only of interest in relation to a set of derived ratings. The principal aim of the study was to predict which individuals would fall prey to depression according to the predefined hypotheses.

It is less usual for qualitative work to be done at the end of, or as a follow-up to, the main (quantitative) project (Sieber, 1973). As Sieber notes, quantitative researchers rarely 'have to hand the additional information required for furthering the study, a methodological embarrassment which may account for the superficiality of a good many reports based on survey analysis' (Sieber, 1973, p.1352). Situations in which qualitative fieldwork postdates quantitative work include: the clarification of a puzzling finding which the quantitative data cannot explain; the emergence of small but interesting sub groups which require more detailed exploration; the need to follow up an issue in a way where it is inappropriate to apply quantitative methods.

The following is an example of 'further clarification'. A survey was carried out of those people who had taken advantage of a cash incentive to move out of council housing. The findings suggested that the majority had moved within a local radius whilst only a handful had moved a long distance. Qualitative methods were then employed in order to find out more about the latter group (Ritchie, personal communication.)

A similar example is cited in Sieber (1973). A study involving surveys of parents, teachers and students had a fieldwork component which was carried out once the surveys had been completed. One of the reasons given by the researchers as to the purpose of the fieldwork was 'curiosity' - in the words of the researchers, 'to see these communities with which we had become so familiar' (Wilder and Friedman, 1968 cited in Sieber, 1973).

The next example involved the use of qualitative methods before as well as after the survey. In a study of Peruvian villages Whyte conducted some exploratory fieldwork on one village. An examination of his fieldnotes revealed that the village was characterised by low levels of conflict and cooperation (Whyte, 1976 cited in Bryman, 1988, p.136). According to the ethnographic literature of the time these two dimensions constituted two ends of a single continuum; they were presumed not to exist in combination. Whyte then revised his theoretical framework in the light of his early fieldnotes by taking account of the finding that conflict and cooperation could be orthogonal to each other. He then tested this new hypothesis out on his survey data. The hypothesis was confirmed, thereby indicating that conflict and cooperation were separate but cross-cutting dimensions. It is reported that he then went on to carry out further ethnographic investigations in order to explore the processual shift between cooperation and conflict.

The pre-eminence of the qualitative over the quantitative

Where quantitative methods are subservient or subsidiary to qualitative ones they tend to fulfil three types of function. First, they provide quantified background data in which to contextualise small scale intensive studies. These are often derived from official statistics, such as census data, or secondary analysis of large scale data sets. A study by Morris (1988) of the social polarisation taking place between households of the employed and unemployed in the North East used a representative sample of addresses from the electoral register as its sampling strategy. The interviews, carried out at all the addresses drawn from the register, also served to provide a quantifiable picture concerning employment and domestic features of the population, against which to interpret the case studies of the employed and unemployed households (Morris, 1988).

Second, quantitative methods may be used in order to test hypotheses thrown up by the qualitative work. However where this occurs the survey part of the study tends to become dominant. An example of qualitative work which subsequently led to a quantitative survey is a study of home workers. This preliminary study was carried out by a different research team from the one which subsequently did the survey (Cragg and Dawson, 1981). Significantly, in the preface to the study (by Hakim), the qualitative study is evaluated according to its statistical rather than its theoretical contribution, namely the size of the 'sample' - 'the largest study so far conducted on this topic, sampling - equal representation of blue-collar and white-collar occupations and so on' (Cragg and Dawson, 1981). The two studies, though clearly linked together, also stand alone (they appear in separate publications) and belong better in the next category in which both methods are given equal emphasis. Since both studies were written up separately, it is not possible to judge their status in relation to each other.

Third, quantitative work may provide a basis for the sampling of cases and comparison groups which form the intensive study. Statistically representative data enable the researcher to decide whether or not it is necessary to sample cases on representative or other criteria. A current study of adolescent health and the parenting of adolescents in which I am involved began with a survey of young people in schools, one of its principal functions being to generate criteria for the selection of households in the main intensive study of households. One useful outcome of surveys is that they can indicate the incidence of particular groups which are of interest in the general population. Where such groups turn out to be small this discovery may then lead the researchers to over-sample them.

Subsidiary quantitative work may be carried out at any point of the research process. A survey may be conducted either as a preliminary to the main qualitative study or at the end of it. Contextual information of a quantified variety may be collected at any point. (Quantitative work which provides a basis for samples must, of necessity, be conducted first.)

It is notable that where the qualitative aspect of the research is pre-eminent the quantitative work is normally conducted by the researchers who are versed in qualitative methods, as was the case in the last study cited.

The qualitative and quantitative are given equal weight

Combined methods may result in two separate but linked studies which are distinct from one another at all stages of the research process. Each study may have a life of its own from the design stage onwards. Alternatively, the methods are integrated in the one study, with the linkage occurring in the fieldwork phase or in the analysis or writing-up stage. The methods may be conducted simultaneously or consecutively. They may be conducted by multi-talented researchers or by separate teams of specialist researchers. Studies under this heading are distinguished by the fact that both types of data figure roughly equally in terms of resources allocated to them and both play an equal part in the analysis and writing-up.

As an example of a project with a combined approach I have chosen one from my own experience. It is relatively unusual in that the project was not conceived in the multi-method paradigm, at least not in the initial conceptualisation. It is an example of a project where the two methods were combined within one fieldwork instrument (see also Chapter 5).

The study was longitudinal in design and multi-disciplinary in organization. Its focus was the experience of mothers returning to full-time employment after the birth of the first child and the effects of this course of action upon mothers and children (Brannen and Moss, 1991). The original conceptualisation of the research was couched in the quantitative paradigm - namely to explore relationships between computed variables, cross-sectionally and over time. Particular attention was to be paid to describing women's mental health and employment behaviour and the child-care arrangements over time. In practice the original aims of the project were fulfilled in terms of the quantitative paradigm.

While in the original proposal there was an emphasis on 'objective' descriptive data and statistical explanations of patterns of behaviour in terms of some pre-defined factors, a new set of concerns was introduced after the research team was recruited. These centred around women's constructions and definitions of the experience of being a mother in full-time employment while having a young child: the process of deciding to return to work, women's experiences of different kinds of social support, the meaning of employment, ways of coping and so on. The theoretical perspective related to these conceptualisations drew upon the sociological theory of phenomenology and social action; the aim was to understand the ways in which women constructed their careers in employment and motherhood in the context of situational and ideological resources. It was thought most appropriate to address these processual issues by means of an intensive interviewing technique in which women would be encouraged to talk at length about their experiences, according to their own definitions rather than fitting their responses to researchers' questions and pre-defined categories.

These techniques were grafted on to the interview schedule so that highly specific pieces of (pre-coded) information were gathered at the same time as more wide-ranging open-ended accounts. The interviewers were trained to probe, to treat the schedule flexibly, to allow the respondent to talk at length and to consider the whole interview in its entirety. In transcribing the tape-recorded material on to the interview schedules the interviewers were also expected to cross-reference related responses to one another.

The twin uses of the interview method for collecting different types of data - one yielding qualitative material (some of which were also subsequently treated quantitatively though not statistically) and the other producing computed quantitative (statistical) data - came into their own in the analysis stage of the project. The two data sets required separate strategies of analysis which proceeded in parallel. (Qualitative analysis was carried out on a subset of the interviews since it was not logistically possible to treat in this way the entire body of data produced by the study.) In general the two types of data were treated as complementary to one another since each data set related to different research questions. However there was also some overlap in the treatment of the data. By this I mean that some questions that were essentially to do with social processes and respondents' definitions were also coded according to the quantitative paradigm and processed accordingly. In some of these cases the data produced findings that appeared consistent with the qualitative data. In other cases there was inconsistency, an outcome upon which the qualitative data were especially illuminating.

An example of inconsistent data concerns women's reported satisfaction with husbands. According to the quantitative data (a coded response to one general question), women in these dual-earner households appeared to be fairly satisfied with their husbands' contribution to housework and child care in spite of the fact that these were far from equally shared. This was surprising since the workload of combining a full-time job with caring for a young baby was a heavy one, plus the fact that women subscribed unequivocally to the view that the domestic workload ought to be shared. When we examined the qualitative material, however, we noted a greater propensity on the part of women to criticise their partners, if only implicitly, especially when their accounts focused on particular incidents. We also noticed that critical comments were played down, retracted or balanced out with favourable comments, especially when women were confronted, in the context of describing what were obvious difficulties in their lives, with direct questions requiring global, evaluative responses. The analysis of their excuses was suggestive of the continuing influence of dominant ideologies of male breadwinners and full-time motherhood (Brannen and Moss, 1991).

In this study the quantitative and qualitative components of the research proceeded alongside one another. The qualitative component was introduced at the fieldwork stage of the research and, in the writing-up, both approaches were accorded equal weight. In general they addressed different but associated questions so that the two types of data complemented one another. Where they addressed the same questions any inconsistencies found were illuminated by the qualitative material. Both data sets were used for descriptive and explanatory purposes. Cases were also used in the text in order to indicate the dynamics of social process rather than as illustrations. The approach drew attention to an advantage of the multi-method approach, namely its ability to confront contradictions and highlight the fragmented and multi-faceted nature of human consciousness. This benefit is one which supercedes the commonly acclaimed advantage of increasing data validity.

Conclusion

The chapter has considered what are commonly assumed to be the main differences between qualitative and quantitative paradigms. It has drawn attention to ways in which the paradigms overlap and ways in which they differ. It has shown that there is considerable overlap in the processes of logical enquiry which underpin them. Where the approaches differ most is in their methods, their (often presumed) relation to theory and their treatment of data as knowledge.

The chapter then went on to outline the methodology of combining qualitative and quantitative approaches and to consider some of the theoretical implications of this strategy. It was suggested that, in so far as the use of different research methods is underpinned by different sets of ideas - about the nature of data, theories about the social world and so on - it is inappropriate to seek to integrate data sets produced by different methods. Rather the researcher should seek to relate each set of data to the theory underpinning it and to see in what ways the data sets complement and contradict one another.

The practical context in which research methods are selected and employed were also considered. The context includes the predilections of funders and the established preferences of policy makers concerning what are appropriate data and methods, together with constraints within academic disciplines and the research community itself.   Particular attention was paid to the nature of the research career in Britain and the social organization of the research team. In addition political perspectives and values were noted as a significant force which determines choice of paradigms. The adoption of a multi-method approach is one which is especially likely to force researchers to consider the practical constraints on the research process.

The paper concluded with a discussion of the various ways in which qualitative and quantitative methods were combined within research projects, with reference to specific examples. Attention was paid to the priority given to the respective approaches within a research project, their time ordering and the stage in the research process at which they were introduced or ceased to figure.

By way of conclusion a few personal observations may be made about the process of considering these issues. While writing about them I have experienced a constant buffeting between the ideals about the way research ought to be done and the very real constraints of the social context. The methodology literature and my own inclination constantly forced me back to consider philosophical questions - theoretical assumptions and their connection with particular paradigms concerning the nature of data as knowledge. On the other hand, in the many discussions I have had with researchers on this topic and in considering the written reports of research, I have been struck by the pragmatic factors which play a part in determining choice of methods. In particular I have been struck by the force of habit, by an unspoken maxim that, as it were, 'the way one begins is the way one continues.' Such impressions suggest that a powerful knowledge paradigm becomes, even if it does not start out that way, a taken-for-granted set of ideas rather than a persistent self-conscious embrace of them.

I have also been struck both by the small amount of literature on combining methods and the relatively few studies which have adopted this strategy. (Even fewer researchers have written about it.) This seems to me a pity since, as I would now argue, far from inducing theoretical eclecticism, a multi-method strategy can have quite the opposite effect. Indeed it can serve as an exercise in clarification: in particular it can help to clarify the formulation of the research problem and the most appropriate ways in which problems or aspects of problems may be theorised and studied. With a single method the researcher is not forced to consider these issues in quite the same way. With multiple methods the researcher has to confront the tensions between different theoretical perspectives while at the same time considering the relationship between the data sets produced by the different methods.

Although, as I have indicated, there may well be more overlap between qualitative and quantitative paradigms, especially in the logic of enquiry, than is commonly assumed, I would still argue in favour of retaining some elements of the dichotomy. For some purposes it is useful to think in terms of opposites if only, in this case, to guard against a creeping pragmatism and an absence of theoretical perspective. Certainly the process of considering these issues has given me a new set of spectacles through which I have seen, with a sudden clarity and freshness, those 'deep down things' - the main issues of the research endeavour, namely the relationship between theory, methods and data.

Acknowledgements

I should especially like to acknowledge the useful discussions I had on this topic with Jane Ritchie, Carolyn Davies and Barbara Tizard and also the extensive and very helpful comments on the paper made by Martyn Hammersley. Thanks are also due to Alan Bryman.

References

Abrams, P., Deem, R., Finch, J., Rock, P. (eds) (1981) *Practice and Progress: British Sociology 1950-80*. London: George Allen and Unwin.
Berthaux, D. (1981) 'From the life-history approach to the transformation of sociological practice'. In *Biography and Society: The life-history approach in the social sciences*. London: Sage.
Brannen, J. and Moss, P. (1991) *Managing Mothers: Dual earner households after maternity leave*. London: Unwin Hyman.
Brannen, J. and Moss, P. (1988) *New Mothers at Work: Childcare and employment*. London: Unwin Hyman.
Brannen, P. (1987) 'Research and policy - political, organisational and cultural constraints'. In F. Heller (ed.) *The Use and Abuse of Research*. London: Sage.

Brown, G.W. (1988) 'Social factors and the development and course of depressive disorders in women. A review of a research programme'. *British Journal of Social Work, 17,* pp.615-634.

Bryman, A. (1988) *Quantity and Quality in Social Research.* London: Unwin Hyman.

Bryman, A. (1984) 'The debate about quantitative and qualitative research: A question of method or epistemology'. *The British Journal of Sociology, 35,* 1, pp.75-93.

Bulmer, M. (1979) 'Concepts in the analysis of qualitative data'. *Sociological Review, 27,* 4, pp.653-677.

Burgess, R.G. (1984) *In the Field: An introduction to field research.* London: George Allen and Unwin.

Burgess, R.G. (1982) 'Multiple strategies in field research'. In R.G. Burgess (ed.) *Field Research: A sourcebook and field manual.* London: George Allen and Unwin.

Burgess, R.G. (ed.) (1982) *Field Research: A sourcebook and field manual.* London: George Allen and Unwin.

Cain, M. and Finch, J. (1981) 'Towards a rehabilitation of data'. In. P. Abrams, R. Deem, J. Finch and P. Rock (eds) *Practice and Progress: British Sociology 1950-1980.* London: George Allen and Unwin.

Campbell, D.T. and Fiske, D.W. (1959) 'Convergent and discriminant validation by the multitrait-multimethod matrix'. *Psychological Bulletin, 56,* 2, pp.81-105.

Cicourel, A.V. (1981) 'Notes on the integration of micro- and macro-levels of analysis'. In K. Knorr-Cetina and A.V. Cicourel (eds) *Advances in Social Theory and Methodology.* London: Routledge and Kegan Paul.

Clifford, J. (1986) 'Introduction: Partial truths'. In J. Clifford and G.G. Marcus *Writing Culture: The poetics and practice of ethnography.* University of California Press.

Cragg, A. and Dawson, T. (1981) 'Qualitative research among homeworkers'. *Research Paper No. 21.* Department of Employment, May.

Delamont, S. (1981) 'All too familiar? A decade of classroom research'. *Educational Analysis, 3,* 1, pp.69-82.

Denzin, N. (1970) *The Research Act in Sociology.* London: Butterworth.

Fielding, N.G. (ed.) (1988) *Actions and Structure: Research methods and social theory.* London: Sage.

Fielding, N.G. and Fielding, J.L. (1986) *Linking Data: Qualitative Research Network Series 4.* London: Sage.

Finch, J. (1986) *Research and Policy: The uses of qualitative methods in social and educational research.* Lewes: Falmer Press.

Finch, J. (1983) 'It's great to have someone to talk to: The ethics of interviewing women'. In C. Bell and H. Roberts (eds) *Social Researching.* London: Routledge and Kegan Paul.

Giddens, A. (1976) *New Rules of Sociological Method.* London: Hutchinson.

Glaser, B.G. and Strauss, A.L. (1967) *The Discovery of Grounded Theory: Strategies in qualitative research.* New York: Aldine de Gruyter.

Graham, H. (1983) 'Do her answers fit his questions? Women and the survey method'. In E. Gamarnikow, D. Morgan, J. Purvis and D. Taylorson *The Public and the Private.* London: Heinemann.

Halfpenny, P. (1979) 'The analysis of qualitative data'. *Sociological Review, 27,* 4, pp.799-825.

Hammersley, M. (1985) 'From ethnography to theory: A programme and paradigm in the sociology of education'. *Sociology, 19,* 2, pp.244-259.

Hammersley, M. (1989) *The Dilemma of Qualitative Methods: Herbert Blumer and the Chicago Tradition.* London: Routledge and Kegan Paul.

Hammersley, M. and Atkinson, P. (1983) *Ethnography: Principles in practice.* London: Tavistock Publications.

Kay, H. (1989) Constructing the epistemological gap: Gender relations in social research. Paper given to the British Sociological Association, Plymouth, March.

Kendall, P.L. and Wolf, K.M. (1949) 'The analysis of deviant cases in communications research'. In P. Lazersfeld and F.W. Stanton (eds) *Communications Research 1948-49.* New York: Harper.

Knorr-Cetina, K. (1988) 'The micro-social order: Towards a reconception'. In N. Fielding (ed.) *Actions and Structure: Research methods and social theory.* London: Routledge and Kegan Paul.

Knorr-Cetina, K. and Cicourel, A.V. (eds) (1981) *Advances in Social Theory and Methodology: Towards an integration of micro- and macro-sociologies.* London: Routledge and Kegan Paul.

Layder, D. (1988) 'The relation of theory and method: Causal relatedness, historical contingency and beyond'. *Sociological Review, 36,*3, pp.441-463.

Lindesmith, A.R. (1968) *Additives and Opiates.* Chicago: Aldine.

Massey, D. and Allen, J. (1988) *The Economy in Question.* London: Sage Publications.

McCracken, G. (1988) The Long Interview: *Qualitative Research Series*, 13. London: Sage.

Mitchell, C.J. (1983) 'Case and situation analysis'. *Sociological Review*, *31*, 2, pp.187-211.

Morgan, D.H.J. (1981) 'Men, masculinity and the process of sociological enquiry'. In H. Roberts (ed.) *Doing Feminist Research.* London: Routledge and Kegan Paul.

Morris, L.D. (1988) 'Local social polarisation: A case study of Hartlepool'. *International Journal of Urban and Regional Research*

Oakley, A. and Rajan, L. (1991) 'Social class and social support'. *Sociology*, *25*, pp.31-59.

Oakley, A. (1981) 'Interviewing women: A contradiction in terms?'. In H. Roberts (ed.) *Doing Feminist Research.* London: Routledge and Kegan Paul.

Platt, J. (1988) 'What can case studies do?'. *Studies in Qualitative Methodology*, *1*, pp.1-20.

Platt, J. (1986) 'Functionalism and the survey: The relation of theory and method'. *Sociological Review*, *34*, 3, pp.501-536.

Reiss, A.J. (1968) 'Stuff and nonsense about social surveys and participant observation'. In H.S. Becker, B. Geer, D. Reisman and R.S. Weiss (eds) *Institutions and Persons.* Papers presented to Everett C. Hughes. Chicago: Aldine.

Rock, P. (1973) 'Phenomenalism and essentialism in the sociology of deviance'. *Sociology*, *7*, 1, pp.17-29.

Sieber, S.D. (1973) 'The integration of fieldwork and survey methods'. *American Journal of Sociology*, *78*, 6, pp.1335-1359.

Silverman, D. (1985) *Qualitative Methodology and Sociology: Describing the social world.* Aldershot: Gower.

Stacey, M. (1960) *Tradition and Change.* Oxford: Oxford University Press.

Stanley, L. and Wise, S. (1983) *Breaking Out: Feminist consciousness and feminist research.* London: Routledge and Kegan Paul.

Whyte, N.F. (1976) 'Research methods for the study of conflict and co-operation'. *American Sociologist*, *11*, 4, pp.208-216.

Wilder, D.E. and Friedmann, N.S. (1968) 'Selecting ideal-typical communities and gaining access to their schools for social research purposes'. In D.E. Wilder, N.S. Friedmann, R.B. Hill, E.E. Scandis and S.D. Sieber (eds) *Actual and Perceived Consensus on Educational Goals between School and University.* New York Bureau of Applied Social Research, Columbia University.

Yin, R. (1989) *Case Study Research: Design and methods.* Revised Edition. London: Sage.
Znaniecki, F. (1934) *The Method of Sociology.* New York: Farrars and Rinehart.

2 Deconstructing the qualitative-quantitative divide[1]

Martyn Hammersley

Introduction

In this chapter I want to challenge the widely held idea that there are two methodological paradigms in social research: the quantitative and the qualitative. This idea seems to have become a matter of consensus over the past few years among many who see themselves on one side of this divide or the other (and even among some who wish to sit astride it). I shall argue, however, that the distinction between qualitative and quantitative is of limited use and, indeed, carries some danger.

It is striking how prone we are to the use of dichotomies, and how these often come to represent distillations of all that is good and bad. Certainly, 'qualitative' and 'quantitative' are sometimes used to represent fundamentally opposed approaches to the study of the social world, one representing the true way, the other the work of the devil. But even where the evaluative overtones are absent and the two approaches are given parity, the distinction is still misleading in my view because it obscures the breadth of issues and arguments involved in the methodology of social research.

In one form or another, the debate about quantitative and qualitative research has been taking place since at least the mid-nineteenth century. At that time there was much argument about the scientific status of history and the social sciences, with quantification often being seen as one of the key features of natural science.[2] Similarly, in US sociology in the 1920s and 30s there was a dispute between advocates of case study and of statistical method. Many of the claims made about quantitative and qualitative method today have their origins in these earlier debates (see Hammersley, 1989a). By the 1940s and 50s in sociology, psychology and some other fields, quantitative method (in the form of survey and experimental research) had become the dominant approach. But since the 1960s there has been a revival in the fortunes of qualitative types of research in these disciplines, to the point where their legitimacy is widely accepted.[3] In some areas this has led to a détente (Rist, 1977; Smith and Heshusius, 1986) and to increased interest in the combination or even integration of quantitative and qualitative. But such talk still preserves the dichotomy. And it seems to me that in some respects détente is worse than cold war. In learning to live and let live there is the danger that we will all quietly forget the methodological disagreements that we should be tackling.[4]

What I am recommending, then, is not that we should revert from two paradigms to one, in such a way as to deny the variety of ideas, strategies and techniques to be found in social research. Quite the reverse. My aim is to show that this diversity cannot be encapsulated within two (or, for that matter, three, four or more) paradigms. Nor should the variety of approach be regarded as stemming simply from fundamental philosophical or political commitments. Arguments about the latter are, and should be, important in methodology. However, they are not the only considerations that are significant; the particular purposes of the research and the practicality of various strategies given the circumstances in which the inquiry is to be carried out are others. Nor do philosophical and political assumptions have the sort of determinate implications for method that they are sometimes assumed to have.[5]

What I want to do in this chapter is to identify the various component meanings of the qualitative/quantitative distinction, particularly as used by advocates of qualitative research. I shall argue that these issues are not as simple or as closely related as is sometimes believed. I have identified seven such issues here. There may be others, but these are probably the main ones:

1. Qualitative versus quantitative data.
2. The investigation of natural versus artificial settings.
3. A focus on meanings rather than behaviour.
4. Adoption or rejection of natural science as a model.
5. An inductive versus a deductive approach.

6. The identification of cultural patterns as against seeking scientific laws.
7. Idealism versus realism.

Qualitative versus quantitative data

In their book on qualitative data analysis, Miles and Huberman characterize the distinction between qualitative and quantitative research in terms of the use of words rather than numbers (Miles and Huberman, 1984, p.15). While it is rare to find such an interpretation spelled out so clearly, it seems to underlie much talk of qualitative methods. And it is true that research reports do differ sharply in the extent to which tables and statistical analysis, on the one hand, and verbal presentations, on the other, predominate. At the same time, a large proportion of research reports (including many that are regarded as qualitative) combine the two, to varying degrees. More importantly, though, the fact that this is not a very satisfactory basis for the distinction between qualitative and quantitative is illustrated by an exchange that took place in US sociology in the 1930s, between Znaniecki (an advocate of case study) and George Lundberg (a positivistic supporter of statistical method). Znaniecki had written a book in which he largely dismissed the use of statistical techniques in sociology. Here is how Lundberg replies to him:

> The current idea seems to be that if one uses pencil and paper, especially squared paper, and if one uses numerical symbols, especially Arabic notation, one is using quantitative methods. If, however, one discusses masses of data with concepts of 'more' or 'less' instead of formal numbers, and if one indulges in the most complicated correlations but without algebraic symbols, then one is not using quantitative methods.

> A striking illustration from a recent book by a prominent sociologist will make the point clear. After a discussion of the lamentable limitations of statistical methods, the author appends this remarkable footnote: 'Wherever the statistical method definitely gains ascendancy, the number of students of a high intellectual level who are attracted to sociology tends to fall off considerably' (Znaniecki, 1934, p.235). In short, this author finally reverts to a statistical proof of the deplorable effects of statistics. (Lundberg, 1964, pp.59-60).

It has frequently been pointed out that ethnographers regularly make quantitative claims in verbal form, using formulations like 'regularly', 'frequently', 'often', 'sometimes', 'generally', 'in the main', typically', 'not atypically' etc.   And it is fairly obvious, I think, that (as Lundberg indicates) the form in which such claims are made makes no difference to their character.

The contrast between words and numbers does not get us very far, then. But there is an important sort of variation in the nature of data that is not unrelated to the word/number contrast. When quantitative researchers criticise ethnographers' use of words rather than numbers what is usually at issue is precision. They are arguing that ethnographers are insufficiently precise in their claims, and that the necessary precision requires quantification.

However, we must ask what precision is, and whether the most precise formulations are always the best; or, indeed, whether they are always necessary. And I think it is clear that precision does not necessarily mean numbers. For example, where we are concerned with the presence or absence of a particular type of phenomenon in a situation, this can be described quite precisely without the use of numbers.   It is also important to remember that precision is not the only virtue in description and measurement. Accuracy is usually even more important. And it is widely recognized that we should not express our findings in terms that imply a greater degree of precision than their likely accuracy warrants. For instance, to report findings to six figures of decimals is rarely if ever justified in social research. It follows from this that sometimes it may not be legitimate to use terms that are more precise than 'sometimes', 'often', 'generally' etc.[6] Handlin (1979, pp.11-12) provides an illustration of this from history:

> I cannot wholly agree that historical problems that hinge on the question 'how many?' are always better solved by numerical answers. The more precise statement is not always the more accurate one. In 1813 John Adams tried to estimate how many colonists were for independence and hazarded various guesses - nearly equally divided; a third; five to two. It would no doubt be more precise to be able to say 39 per cent were for, 31 per cent against, and 30 per cent neutral, or to plant a good solid decimal point with a long series of digits behind it. But it would be less accurate to do so, for the data does not support that degree of refinement.

Furthermore, while increased precision may often be of value, it is not always so. It may not be of value because the level of precision already achieved is sufficient for our purposes, or because the likely costs of achieving greater precision are greater than the probable benefits. The latter is an especially important point in the context of case study research, where a relatively wide focus is adopted. Given fixed resources, the attempt to make any part of the picture more precise will necessarily tend to reduce the width of focus that is possible. The researcher must judge whether the benefits of this outweigh the costs, and sometimes they will not. Equally, though, on other occasions they will; and more precise, even numerical, descriptions will be appropriate.[7]

We are not faced, then, with a stark choice between words and numbers, or even between precise and imprecise data. Furthermore, our decisions about what level of precision is appropriate in relation to any particular claim should depend on the nature of what we are trying to describe, on the likely accuracy of our descriptions, on our purposes, and on the resources available to us; not on ideological commitment to one methodological paradigm or another.

Investigation of 'natural' versus 'artificial' settings

A second interpretation of the qualitative/quantitative distinction focuses on the nature of the phenomenon investigated: whether it is 'naturally occurring' or has been created by the researcher. The sharpest contrast here is between experiments and ethnographic research. The former involves study of a situation especially established by the researchers, probably using volunteer subjects, and designed to capture different values of some theoretical variables while controlling relevant extraneous variables. Ethnographic research, on the other hand, requires the study of situations that would have occurred without the ethnographer's presence, and the adoption of a role in that situation designed to minimise the researcher's impact on what occurs. In common parlance, experimenters study 'artificial' settings, while ethnographers study 'natural' settings; and the implication is that only the latter is worthwhile because it is 'natural' behaviour we are concerned to understand.

The charge of artificiality may also be directed at formal, structured interviews of the kind used by survey researchers. These may be contrasted with unstructured and/or informal interviews, where the interviewer plays a less dominant role. While the latter do not represent an entirely 'natural' setting, it is often argued that their closeness to ordinary conversation renders them approximations to the natural.

In my view this distinction between natural and artificial settings is spurious. What happens in a school class or in a court of law, for example, is no more natural (or artificial) than what goes on in a social psychological laboratory. To treat classrooms or courtrooms as natural and experiments as artificial is to forget that social research is itself part of the social world, something that should never be forgotten.

Once again, though, there is an important issue implicit in this distinction. What is involved is variation in the degree to which the researcher shapes the data. There is a trade-off between, on the one hand, trying to make sure that one gets the relevant data (in the most efficient manner possible) and, on the other hand, the danger of reactivity, of influencing the people studied in such a way that error is introduced into the data. It has long been a criticism of experiments that their findings do not generalize to the 'real world' (that is to non-experimental situations) because people's behaviour is shaped by their awareness of the experimental situation, and by the personal characteristics of the experimenter (or her/his assistants). Similarly, structured interviews have been criticized because we cannot generalize from what is said in them to what is said and done elsewhere.[8] However, while there is some truth in these arguments, they by no means render the results of research using 'artificial' methods of no value. Much depends on whether the reactivity affects the results in ways that are relevant to the research topic and in ways that cannot be allowed for. All research is subject to potential error of one kind or another. Indeed, even ethnographic research in 'natural' settings is not immune to reactivity. While the ethnographer may strive to minimize her or his effects on the situation studied, no one can guarantee this; and sometimes the effects can be significant despite the researcher's best efforts. Also, we must remember what the significance of reactivity is: it makes the setting investigated unrepresentative of those about which the researcher wishes to generalize, an issue sometimes referred to as ecological invalidity. But reactivity is not the only source of ecological invalidity. Even without reactivity, a natural setting can be unrepresentative because it differs in important ways from most other cases in the same category. Simply choosing to investigate natural settings, and seeking to adopt a low profile in them, does not ensure ecological validity.[9]

For these reasons the distinction between natural and artificial settings does not provide a sound basis for the qualitative/quantitative distinction. The terms 'natural' and 'artificial' have misleading connotations. And while the issue of ecological validity is important, it is not the only important methodological issue. Nor does research in 'natural' settings guarantee ecological validity, any more than research in 'artificial' settings automatically debars us from it.

A focus on meanings versus a focus on behaviour

This component of the qualitative-quantitative distinction emphasizes the interpretive or hermeneutic character of qualitative research. Of all the issues discussed in this chapter, this one links most obviously back to nineteenth century debates about the difference between natural science and history, as well as to twentieth century disputes such as that surrounding behaviourism.

It is sometimes suggested that the central goal of qualitative research is to document the world from the point of view of the people studied (from the native point of view, in Malinowski's terms), rather than presenting it from the perspective of the researcher. And it is true that qualitative research does seek to understand the perspectives of the people studied, on the grounds that this is essential if we are to describe and explain their behaviour effectively. However, it is very rare for qualitative research to restrict itself to documenting the native point of view. And there are good reasons for not doing this; not the least of which is that the people studied can often do this for themselves! Even those approaches that restrict the research focus to participants' perspectives do not simply reproduce these, but seek to analyse their structure and/or production in ways that are likely to be alien to the people studied. This is true, for example, of both ethnosemantics and ethnomethodology. But, as I have said, most qualitative research does not restrict its focus this narrowly. It seeks to describe and explain both perspectives and behaviour, recognizing that the latter does not merely flow from the former, and may even be discrepant with it. Indeed, such ironic discrepancies have been a major focus for qualitative research (see, for example, Keddie, 1971; Sharp and Green, 1975; and Willis, 1977).

Conversely, much quantitative research is concerned with attitudes rather than simply with behaviour. Advocates of an interpretive approach may argue that attitude research effectively studies attitudes as behaviour displayed in response to interview questions. Yet, critiques of behaviourism emphasise that it is not possible to study human behaviour without attributing meanings, and that behaviourists routinely do this despite themselves. Given this fact, it seems that attitude researchers cannot but be studying 'meanings'. At the very least, this shifts the criticism elsewhere. Moreover, most attitude researchers do not operate on the basis of a strict behaviourism.

It is still true, of course, that there are differences between attitude researchers and qualitative sociologists, both in how they conceptualize the meanings held to underlie behaviour, and in how they seek to identify those meanings. Even here, though, the differences are not as great as is sometimes suggested. It is common for ethnographers to ascribe perspectives or definitions of the situation to the people they study, and it is not clear how these differ in character from attitudes. Ethnographers may stress that they do not assume a mechanical relationship between attitude and behaviour. However, the more contingent is the relationship between perspective and behaviour, the less value perspectives have as explanatory factors. So this is not an argument that ethnographers can pursue very far without undercutting the basis of their own hermeneutic approach.

As regards differences in the approach that attitude researchers and ethnographers employ in identifying attitudes/perspectives, the contrast is between the use of attitude scales and more unstructured approaches. As such, it reduces to the previous two distinctions I have already discussed, and to the distinction between inductive and deductive approaches that I shall deal with below. Here again, though, we do not have a clear-cut distinction between two contrasting approaches.

Natural science as a model

It is common for quantitative method to be criticised for taking natural science as its model. It is worth noting, however, that advocates of qualitative method have sometimes themselves regarded the natural sciences as exemplary. Thomas and Znaniecki, two of the most influential advocates of case study and life history methods in the 1920s and 30s, make the following comment at the beginning of their study of *The Polish Peasant in Poland and America:*

The marvellous results attained by rational technique (that is, by science) in the sphere of material reality invite us to apply some analogous procedure to social reality. Our success in controlling nature gives us confidence that we shall eventually be able to control the social world in the same measure (Thomas and Znaniecki, 1927, p.1).

Nor were Thomas and Znaniecki unusual in holding this view. While he was uncertain about the chances of its achievement, Herbert Blumer was also committed, at least in the 1920s and early 30s, to the pursuit of a science of society modelled on the natural sciences. Much the same was true in social anthropology. Boas, Malinowski and Radcliffe-Brown all took the natural sciences as a paradigm for their approach to the study of primitive society; though, as in the case of Blumer and the Chicago sociologists, this was tempered with ideas about the distinctiveness of social phenomena (Hammersley, 1989a).

From a historical point of view, then, differences in attitude to natural science do not seem to map on to the distinction between quantitative and qualitative research in a straightforward way. And, even today, there are advocates of qualitative method who justify their approach precisely on the basis of its similarity to that of natural scientists.[10]

What this points to is that the issue of whether natural science is an appropriate model for social research is not a simple one. There are at least three complications.

First, we must consider which natural science we are taking as the model, and during which period of its development? There are significant differences, for example, between physics and biology; and, indeed, within each natural science discipline over time.

Second, which interpretation of the methods of natural science is to be adopted? Keat and Urry (1975) identify positivist, conventionalist, or realistic interpretations of physics; and even these distinctions do not exhaust the variety of views to be found among philosophers of science.

Third, what aspects of natural science method are to be treated as generic? Not even the most extreme positivist would argue that the methods of physics should be applied lock, stock and barrel to the study of the social world. And there are few supporters of qualitative research who would insist that there is no aspect of natural science method that is relevant to social research. What is involved here is a matter of degree. Once again, we have a complex set of considerations that resist reduction to a simple contrast.

Inductive versus deductive approaches

It is common for qualitative researchers to contrast their own inductive approach with the deductive, or hypothetico-deductive, method of quantitative research. Here too, though, we have an over-simplification. Not all quantitative research is concerned with hypothesis-testing. Many surveys are straightforwardly descriptive, and some quantitative research is explicitly concerned with theory generation. Equally, by no means all ethnographers reject the hypothetico-deductive method.[11]) Indeed, it seems to me that all research involves both deduction and induction in the broad sense of those terms; in all research we move from ideas to data as well as from data to ideas. What is true is that one can distinguish between studies that are primarily exploratory, being concerned with generating theoretical ideas, and those which are more concerned with testing hypotheses. But these types of research are not alternatives; we need both. Nor need the former be quantitative and the latter qualitative in other senses of those terms.

A common version of the inductive versus deductive contrast is built into advocacy Verstehen or understanding, as opposed to forms of explanation that rely on observation of the external features of human behaviour.[12] In its most extreme formulation, Verstehen involves some kind of direct contact with the experience of others, or a reliving of it on the basis of one's own experience. Some versions place great importance on the nature of the relationship between researcher and researched, perhaps regarding equality as essential if understanding is to occur. But while there is no doubt that it is important in research to take account of one's own cultural assumptions and to open them up to possible disconfirmation, the idea that Verstehen involves direct contact with social reality or with other people must be rejected. We can never entirely escape our own assumptions about the world.[13] And even in face-to-face contact with people with whom we share a lot, we are not given knowledge that is necessarily beyond reasonable doubt. As has often been stressed in the ethnographic literature, there are advantages and disadvantages to closeness. On the one hand, it may provide us with inside information that we would otherwise not gain, both about what happens and about people's experiences of events. On the other hand, through a process of over-rapport we may come to take over false assumptions held by the people we are studying, and become unable to see the world in any other way than that in which it appears to them.

Only if we assume that the perspectives of those we are studying necessarily embody genuine knowledge about the world is over-rapport not a danger. And in my view no individual or group has such a monopoly on truth.

From this point of view, then, we cannot but rely on constructing hypotheses, assessing them against experience and modifying them where necessary. This is true whether we engage in hypothesis testing in a formal, explicit and narrow way that involves subjecting hypotheses to crucial tests; or whether we adopt a more informal approach in which we sacrifice some of the sharpness of the test for a more wide-ranging approach in which we allow more of our assumptions to be thrown open to challenge. Furthermore, which of these approaches is most appropriate depends on our purposes, and the stage that our research has reached, not on paradigmatic commitments.

Identifying cultural patterns versus pursuing scientific laws

Following on from the contrast between qualitative and quantitative approaches in terms of a commitment to the model of natural science is the idea that these approaches differ in their goals. Quantitative research is often believed to be committed to the discovery of scientific laws; whereas qualitative research is concerned with identifying cultural patterns. However, as I pointed out in the previous section, much quantitative research is concerned with description rather than with theory development and testing. And, indeed, rather more survey research may appear to be concerned with discovering theoretical laws than is actually the case because survey researchers sometimes fail to distinguish between this goal and that of explaining particular events or relationships.[14]

Similarly, while it is common these days for qualitative researchers to deny the possibility of scientific laws, this was not always so. In the early decades of this century case-study researchers often justified their approach on the grounds that it could produce laws, whereas statistical method could only produce probabilistic generalizations (Blumer, 1928; Znaniecki, 1934). Even today qualitative researchers often claim that their goal is theory rather than the mere description of cultural patterns. And sometimes the concept of theory involved seems to be not far removed from that characteristic of survey research; though it should be said that there is considerable uncertainty about the precise nature of ethnographic theory (Hammersley, 1992, Chapters 1 and 2). Furthermore, both analytic induction and grounded theorising seem to depend on the assumption of laws. For instance, analytic induction involves reconstructing theories when counter examples are discovered. However, this is only sensible if we assume that theories consist of deterministic laws that apply to all cases. Thus the distinction between identifying patterns and pursuing laws seems to provide little clear basis for the division between quantitative and qualitative methods.

Idealism versus realism

At the most abstract philosophical level it has been claimed that qualitative and quantitative researchers are committed to different epistemological positions. A clear example of this argument is to be found in the writings of John K. Smith. He argues that quantitative research is wedded to a realist epistemology in the sense of assuming that true accounts correspond to how things really are and that competing accounts must be judged in terms of whether the procedures adopted ensure accurate representation of reality. By contrast, qualitative method is idealist, he claims, in that it rejects any possibility of representing reality. It recognizes that there may be 'as many realities as there are persons' (Smith, 1984, p.386).

I think it can be shown with little difficulty that this characterisation is inaccurate empirically. First, not all quantitative researchers are realists. Take the following quotation:

> In any valid epistemological or scientific sense we must say that the substitution of a Copernican for the Ptolemaic theory of the universe represented a major change in the universe. To say that it was not the universe but our conception of it which changed is merely a verbal trick designed to lead the unwary into the philosophical quagmires of Platonic realism, for obviously the only universe with which science can deal is our 'conception' of it.

What we have here is an idealist account of natural science knowledge in which there is a denial that it can represent some independent reality. But it does not come from a qualitative researcher. It comes from George Lundberg again, positivist advocate of quantitative method in the 1930s, 40s and 50s (Lundberg, 1933, p.309). There was a strong element of phenomenalism in late nineteenth and twentieth century positivism, and Lundberg's anti-realism reflects this. By contrast, Herbert Blumer's influential concept of naturalistic method is quite clearly realist in character: he talks of research being concerned with discovering the nature of social reality, of tearing away the veil of our preconceptions so that we may see it (Hammersley, 1989a). In more recent times, Harré has based his advocacy and practice of qualitative research in social psychology on an explicit realism.[15] And, indeed, the reliance of ethnography on realism has come under increasing criticism, for example from those who stress the creative character of ethnographic writing (see Tyler, 1985 and Clifford, 1988).

More important than the empirical question of whether it is true that quantitative researchers are realists and qualitative researchers idealists, though, is the philosophical issue of whether there is any necessary connection between qualitative method and a particular epistemological position. As I have shown, history suggests that there is little reason to believe that there is such a connection. And we must remember that there are many more than two epistemological positions available within philosophy, nor can these be reduced to a single dichotomy without great distortion.[16]

Conclusion

In this chapter I have looked at some of the components of the conventional distinction between qualitative and quantitative method. In each case I have argued that what is involved is not a simple contrast between two opposed standpoints, but a range of positions sometimes located on more than one dimension. It should also be clear, I think, that there is no necessary relationship between adopting a particular position on one issue and specific positions on the others. Many combinations are quite reasonable. Furthermore, I emphasized that selection among these positions ought often to depend on the purposes and circumstances of the research, rather than being derived from methodological or philosophical commitments. This is because there are trade-offs involved. For instance, if we seek greater precision we are likely to sacrifice some breadth of description; and vice versa. And the costs and benefits of various trade-off positions will vary according to the particular goals and circumstances of the research being pursued.

What all this implies is that the distinction between quantitative and qualitative approaches does not capture the full range of options that we face; and that it misrepresents the basis on which decisions should be made. What is involved is not a crossroads where we have to go left or right. A better analogy is a complex maze where we are repeatedly faced with decisions, and where paths wind back on one another. The prevalence of the distinction between qualitative and quantitative method tends to obscure the complexity of the problems that face us and threatens to render our decisions less effective than they might otherwise be.

Notes

1.   My use of the term 'deconstructing' in the title of this chapter is no more than a rhetorical flourish: my philosophical assumptions are very different from those of deconstructionists. However, given their views about meaning, they can have no justifiable complaint against my theft of this term! For an excellent critique of deconstructionism, see Ellis 1989. See also Dews, 1987.

2.   This debate has persisted within history, indeed it has intensified in recent years as a result of the growth of 'cliometrics'. For contrasting perspectives on this development see Fogel and Elton, 1983.

3.   For a useful discussion of the current state of this debate, see Bryman, 1988.

4.   To this extent I am in agreement with Smith and Heshusius, but I disagree with much of the rest of what they say. In my view the commitment to paradigms, in whatever form, tends to close down the debate rather than keep it open (Hammersley, 1989b).

5.   This is illustrated by the debates about methodology among Marxists and feminists. See, for example, the debate about Marxism and method in the *Berkeley Journal of Sociology*, *35*, 1989, especially the articles by Wright and Burawoy. On feminism and method, see the very different views expressed by Mies, Jayaratne, Reinharz, and Stanley and Wise in Bowles and Klein (1983).

6.   My own use of imprecise formulations will not be lost on the reader!

7.   There is also the practical question of how much precision is possible. While I would not want to suggest any insuperable barriers to increased precision of measurement of social phenomena, there is no doubt that as things presently stand there are severe practical limits to the level of combined precision and accuracy that can be achieved.

8.   In some respects this is a misleading argument since it fails to draw the necessary distinction between, on the one hand, inferring from what people do in interviews to what they do elsewhere, and, on the other, the question of the truth of what people say in interviews about what they and others do elsewhere.

9.   Equally, it is worth noting that some quantitative researchers carry out their research in natural settings, notably in the form of systematic observational research.

10.   See, for example, the work of Harré: Harré, 1970; Harré and Secord, 1972.

11.   On exploratory quantitative analysis, see Baldamus, 1979 for an example; Erickson and Nosanchuk, 1979 for techniques. Some practitioners of analytic induction (such as Lindesmith, 1937) and of grounded theorizing (Strauss, 1987) explicitly equate their approach with the hypothetico-deductive method.

12.   Platt (1985) points out that Weber's discussion of Verstehen seems to have had little influence on early qualitative researchers. However, Weber drew the concept from earlier nineteenth century discussions, notably those of Dilthey, and these did have an influence on Chicago sociologists; both directly, and indirectly, through Windelband, Rickert and Simmel, for example. It also seems likely that Cooley, who was quite influential on the Chicagoans, drew his concept of sympathetic introspection from the German Romantics.

13.   This is the conclusion of more sophisticated versions of hermeneutics, notably that of Gadamer.

14.   On this distinction, see Hammersley, 1992, Chapter 2.

15.   See Note 7.

16.   For a development of the argument in this section dealing specifically with Smith's position, see Hammersley, 1989b.

References

Baldamus, W. (1979) 'Alienation, anomie and industrial accidents.' In M. Wilson (ed.) *Social and Educational Research in Action.* London: Longman.
Blumer, H. (1928) Method in social psychology. Unpublished PhD dissertation, University of Chicago.
Bowles, G. and Klein, R.D. (1983) *Theories of Women's Studies.* London: Routledge and Kegan Paul.
Bryman, A. (1988) *Quality and Quantity in Social Research.* London: Unwin Hyman.
Clifford, J. (1988) *The Predicament of Culture.* Cambridge, Massachussetts: Harvard University Press.
Dews. P. (1987) *Logics of Disintegration: post-structuralist thought and the claims of critical theory.* London: Verso.
Ellis, J. (1989) *Against Deconstruction.* Princeton: Princeton University Press.
Erickson, B. and Nosanchuk, T. (1979) *Understanding Data: an introduction to exploratory and confirmatory data analysis for students in the social sciences.* Milton Keynes: Open University Press.
Fogel, R.W. and Elton, G.R. (1983) *Which Road to the Past.* New Haven: Yale University Press.
Hammersley, M. (1989a) *The Dilemma of Qualitative Method: Herbert Blumer and the Chicago tradition.* London: Routledge.
Hammersley, M. (1989b) 'The methodology of ethnomethodology', unpublished paper.
Hammersley, M. (1990) Keeping the conversation open: a response to Smith and Heshusius. Unpublished paper.

Hammersley, M. (1992) *What's Wrong with Ethnography? Methodological explorations*. London: Routledge.

Handlin, O. (1979) *Truth in History*. Cambridge, Massachussetts: Harvard University Press.

Harré, R. (1970) *The Principles of Scientific Thinking*. London: Macmillan.

Harré, R. and Secord, P. (1972) *The Explanation of Social Behaviour*. Oxford: Blackwell.

Keat, R. and Urry, J. (1975) *Social Theory as Science*. London: Routledge and Kegan Paul.

Keddie, N. (1971) 'Classroom knowledge.' In M.F.D. Young (ed.) *Knowledge and Control*. New York: Collier Macmillan.

Lindesmith, A. (1937) *The Nature of Opiate Addiction*. Chicago: University of Chicago Libraries.

Lundberg, G. (1933) 'Is sociology too scientific?' *Sociologus*, *9*, 298-322.

Lundberg, G. (1964) *Foundations of Sociology*. New York: McKay.

Miles, M.B. and Huberman, M. (1984) *Qualitative Data Analysis*. Beverly Hills: Sage.

Platt, J. (1985) 'Weber's *Verstehen* and the history of qualitative research: the missing link.' *British Journal of Sociology*, *36*, 3, 448-466.

Rist, R. (1977) 'On the relations among educational research paradigms: from disdain to détente.' *Anthropology and Education Quarterly*, *8*, 2, 42-49.

Sharp, R. and Green, A. (1975) *Education and Social Control*. London: Routledge and Kegan Paul.

Smith, J.K. (1984) 'The problem of criteria for judging interpretive inquiry.' *Educational Evaluation and Policy Analysis*, *6*, 4. 379-391.

Smith, J.K. and Heshusius, L. (1986) 'Closing down the conversation: the end of the quantitative-qualitative debate among educational inquirers.' *Educational Researcher*, *15*, 1, 4-12.

Strauss, A. (1987) *Qualitative Analysis for Social Scientists*. Cambridge: Cambridge University Press.

Thomas, W.I. and Znaniecki, F. (1927) *The Polish Peasant in Europe and America*, five volumes. Chicago: University of Chicago Press/Boston: Badger Press.

Tyler, S.A. (1985) 'Ethnography, intertextuality, and the end of description.' *American Journal of Semiotics*, *3*, 4, 83-98.

Willis, P. (1977) *Learning to Labour*. Farnborough: Saxon House.

Znaniecki, F. (1934) *The Method of Sociology*. New York: Farrar and Rinehart.

3 Quantitative and qualitative research: further reflections on their integration

Alan Bryman

Interest in the differences between quantitative research and qualitative research (or the alternative labels with which these approaches are often served) continues unabated. In the relatively short period since my previous work on this subject (Bryman, 1988) went off to the publisher, the specific issues of the nature of quantitative and qualitative research and their integration have received the attentions of a number of writers, including Laurie and Sullivan (1991), McLaughlin (1991) and three contributors to Stanley's (1990) book on feminist praxis. The nature of quantitative and qualitative research has been a focus within discussions of the prospects for multi-method research generally (Brewer and Hunter, 1989) and has been a significant element within discussions of paradigms in the social sciences (for example, Hoshmand, 1989, and the contributors to Guba, 1990b). Among educational researchers such as Firestone (1987) and Howe (1988) there has been continued evidence of interest in the extent to which quantitative and qualitative research can be combined following Smith and Heshusius's (1986) article on this issue. Clearly, the debate about the nature and differences between these two approaches to social research continues to be of concern to social scientists, though there is considerable disagreement over certain fundamental issues such as the possibility of integrating them. Moreover, a number of different terms have been employed to describe approaches to social research that seem to correspond closely to the quantitative/qualitative contrast. Table 1 attempts to identify some of the major labels that have been used to refer to approaches to research which correspond to quantitative and qualitative research.

Table 1 Quantitative and Qualitative Research: Alternative Labels

Quantitative	Qualitative	Authors
Rationalistic	Naturalistic	Guba & Lincoln (1982)
Inquiry from the outside	Inquiry from the inside	Evered & Louis (1981)
Functionalist	Interpretive	Burrell & Morgan (1979)
Positivist	Constructivist	Guba (1990a)
Positivist	Naturalistic-ethnographic	Hoshmand (1989)

As noted in Bryman (1988), discussions of the two approaches operate at different levels of analysis and discourse. Fundamentally, these can be reduced to two forms. Some writers prefer to identify quantitative and qualitative research (or their synonyms) as distinctive epistemological positions and hence divergent approaches to what is and should count as valid knowledge (for example, Smith and Heshusius, 1986). Such writers sometimes use the term 'paradigm' to refer to each of the two positions though they do not always use it in the sense that Kuhn (1970) implied. Examples of the use of the term paradigm are Burrell and Morgan (1979), Hoshmand (1989), and Guba (1990b). The conception of quantitative and qualitative research as each underpinned by a distinct epistemological position has implications for the question of whether they can genuinely be combined or whether they are irreconcilable.

The view taken here is that quantitative and qualitative research represent distinctive approaches to social research. Each approach is associated with a certain cluster of methods of data collection: quantitative research is strongly associated with social survey techniques like structured interviewing and self-administered questionnaires,

Considerations using multi-methods 59

experiments, structured observation, content analysis, the analysis of
official statistics and the like. Qualitative research is typically associated
with participant observation, semi- and unstructured interviewing, focus
groups, the qualitative examination of texts, and various language-based
techniques like conversation and discourse analysis.

It is true that certain epistemological and theoretical positions have
influenced the character of both quantitative and qualitative research.
The former has clearly been influenced by the natural science model of
research, and its positivist form in particular. Qualitative research has
been influenced by an epistemological position that rejects the
appropriateness of a natural science approach to the study of humans;
this position finds its expression in such theoretical strands as
phenomenology and symbolic interactionism. These epistemological
precursors have influenced the concerns of the two research approaches:
the concern in quantitative research about causality, measurement,
generalizability etc. can be traced back to its natural science roots; the
concern in qualitative research for the point of view of the individuals
being studied, the detailed elucidation of context, the sensitivity to
process, etc., can be attributed to its epistemological roots (Bryman,
1988). But this is not to say that quantitative and qualitative research
are forever rooted to their original epistemological positions. Instead,
the two approaches to research can have and do have an independence
from their epistemological beginnings. As general approaches to social
research, each has its own strengths and weaknesses as an approach to
the conduct of social research. It is these strengths and weaknesses that
lie behind the rationale for integrating them.

Approaches to integrating quantitative and qualitative research

In Bryman (1988, Chapter 6), a number of different ways in which
quantitative and qualitative research have been combined in published
research were outlined. The following is a simple summary of the
approaches that were identified.

1. The logic of 'triangulation'

The findings from one type of study can be checked against the findings
deriving from the other type. For example, the results of a qualitative

investigation might be checked against a quantitative study. The aim is generally to enhance the validity of findings.

2. Qualitative research facilitates quantitative research

Qualitative research may: help to provide background information on context and subjects; act as a source of hypotheses; and aid scale construction.

3. Quantitative research facilitates qualitative research

Usually, this means quantitative research helping with the choice of subjects for a qualitative investigation.

4. Quantitative and qualitative research are combined in order to provide a general picture

Quantitative research may be employed to plug the gaps in a qualitative study which arise because, for example, the researcher cannot be in more than one place at any one time. Alternatively, it may be that not all issues are amenable solely to a quantitative investigation or solely to a qualitative one.

5. Structure and process

Quantitative research is especially efficient at getting to the 'structural' features of social life, while qualitative studies are usually stronger in terms of 'processual' aspects. These strengths can be brought together in a single study.

6. Researchers' and subjects' perspectives

Quantitative research is usually driven by the researcher's concerns, whereas qualitative research takes the subject's perspective as the point of departure. These emphases may be brought together in a single study.

7. The problem of generality

The addition of some quantitative evidence may help to mitigate the fact that it is often not possible to generalize (in a statistical sense) the findings deriving from qualitative research.

8. Qualitative research may facilitate the interpretation of relationships between variables

Quantitative research readily allows the researcher to establish relationships among variables, but is often weak when it comes to exploring the reasons for those relationships. A qualitative study can be used to help explain the factors underlying the broad relationships that are established.

9. The relationship between 'macro' and 'micro' levels

Employing both quantitative and qualitative research may provide a means of bridging the macro-micro gulf. Quantitative research can often tap large-scale, structural features of social life, while qualitative research tends to address small-scale, behavioural aspects. When research seeks to explore both levels, integrating quantitative and qualitative research may be necessary.

10. Stages in the research process

Quantitative and qualitative research may be appropriate to different stages of a longitudinal study.

11. Hybrids

The chief example tends to be when qualitative research is conducted within a quasi-experimental (i.e. quantitative) research design.

It is unlikely that this list can be considered truly exhaustive, though it does represent a fairly comprehensive catalogue. Moreover, any piece of research can exhibit more than one of these approaches to integration.

Observations about the integration of quantitative and qualitative research

What follows is an examination of a number of issues that the foregoing list of approaches to integration throws up. They represent a mixture of plain observations and concerns, with the latter having the function of injecting a sense of caution into the somewhat over-enthusiastic discussions that are sometimes encountered.

Variable frequency of approaches to integration

It should not be concluded that the various approaches to integration are found in equal number. For example, while there are quite a few illustrations of qualitative research acting as a precursor to quantitative research, such as where the former generates hypotheses for subsequent testing by the latter (approach no. 2), there are very few examples where it works the other way around (approach no. 3). By and large, when quantitative research precedes qualitative research it is not in the sense of providing substantive themes that are then followed up with qualitative research. Instead, the role of quantitative research tends to be to facilitate the selection of subjects for semi- or unstructured interviews, which follow on from a large-scale survey. In addition to the example of Kahl (1953) that was cited in Bryman (1988), Blumstein and Schwartz's (1983) research on American couples provides an illustration. These researchers collected quantitative data on social and sexual relationships between couples from 12,000 individuals by postal questionnaire. In addition, they wanted more detailed information from their respondents on a number of issues. They carried out in-depth interviews on 300 couples who were selected from the survey sample in terms of three criteria: whether married, cohabiting, gay males, or lesbians; how long each couple had been together; and level of education. This approach to selecting informants for qualitative-style interviews allowed a range of contrasts between the resulting groups to be drawn.

One way in which approach no. 3 can be brought about in a more substantive way (i.e. not simply the provision of subsets of respondents) is if the integration is conceived in terms of separate investigations. We tend to think of the integration of quantitative and qualitative research in the context of a single study, but there may be circumstances in which it occurs across investigations. In my own research with a number of colleagues some years ago, we were examining the leadership orientations of construction project managers, using a conventional structured interview approach. Such research is helpful in allowing the researcher to determine how far certain situational factors influence leader behaviour and its impact on organizational effectiveness (for example, Bryman et al., 1987). However, the situational factors that we examined were fairly broadly conceptualized, as is generally the case in such leadership research (Bryman, 1992, Chapter 1). A qualitative study was undertaken at a later stage by semi-structured interviews. This study allowed the significance of these factors in the specific context of the construction industry and its project-based structure to be etched with greater sensitivity (Bryman et al., 1988).

The various approaches to integration are not employed with anywhere near equal frequency. The observation that integration need not be considered solely in relation to single projects should also be borne in mind.

The significance of triangulation

The context within which the integration of quantitative and qualitative research is most frequently encountered is in terms of triangulation. Indeed, Brewer and Hunter's (1989) book depicts multi-method research in general, and the integration of quantitative and qualitative research in particular, almost exclusively in terms of triangulation. The notion of triangulation is drawn from the idea of 'multiple operationism' which suggests that the validity of findings and the degree of confidence in them will be enhanced by the deployment of more than one approach to data collection (for example, Webb et al., 1966). These views were originally formulated in the context of quantitative research where more than one approach to operationalizing concepts was essentially being recommended to take account of the fact that all measures are prone to error. The multi-method multi-trait matrix was an early attempt to induce social scientists to reduce their reliance on single-method measures of concepts (Campbell and Fiske, 1959).

In spite of its intuitive appeal, the suggestion that quantitative and qualitative research may be combined for the purposes of triangulation is by no means as unproblematic as it first appears. Three points can be raised. First, it is quite feasible to construct an argument that suggests that the multiple operationism analogy is inappropriate. When a researcher employs, say, both structured interviews and self-administered questionnaires to measure and hence to triangulate core concepts, the methods have similar aims (i.e. to generate measures that can be analyzed statistically) and are broadly comparable. However, quantitative and qualitative research have different preoccupations and highly contrasting strengths and weaknesses. The very fact that the quantitative approach emphasizes causality, variables, and a heavily pre-structured approach to research, while qualitative research is concerned with the elucidation of subjects' perspectives, process, and contextual detail (Bryman, 1988) means that the ensuing data may not be as comparable as is sometimes proposed by the advocates of triangulation. In other words, it is highly questionable whether quantitative and qualitative research are tapping the same things even when they are examining apparently similar issues. Thus, when Weinstein (1979) compared quantitative and qualitative research on mental patients, he found that they came up with very contrasting findings, with quantitative researchers providing a more favourable portrayal of the experience of hospitalization. A critique of his article argued that the qualitative research was concerned with the experience of being a mental patient, whereas the quantitative research was concerned with the attitudes of mental patients (Essex et al., 1990). In other words, there may be some dispute about whether they can genuinely be compared. With the other approaches to integration that were outlined above, this specific issue does not arise because the researcher is interested in bringing together the different concerns and strengths and weaknesses of quantitative and qualitative research.

Second, if a researcher finds that his or her qualitative evidence does not confirm the quantitative results (or vice versa) how should the researcher respond? There is a tendency for researchers to regard their qualitative evidence as more trustworthy than their quantitative data. Thus, in his study of Suffolk farmers, Newby (1977, p. 127) notes that 'where survey and participant observation data conflicted [he] instinctively trusted the latter'. Similar privileged treatments of qualitative data can be found in Faules (1982) and Shapiro (1973). Qualitative research entails the investigator getting close to his or her subjects and being sensitive to the context, and these attributes tend to breed greater confidence in the validity of qualitative data over the quantitative, which may appear by contrast rather superficial. However, this is a very arbitrary criterion for deciding which set of findings should be plumped for, and instead researchers should treat inconsistent findings as suggestive of new lines of enquiry.

A third difficulty is knowing what a conflict in results actually comprises. It is fairly rare for one set of findings to confirm the other set in their entirety. It is often found that the qualitative findings imply a need to qualify the bland quantitative results or that they generated some additional information. For example, Faules (1982) conducted a study of performance appraisal in a US local government organization. He used both a self-administered questionnaire which was handed to 250 employees and conducted semi-structured interviews with 62 employees in order to elicit stories about appraisal. Both approaches were concerned with contentious aspects of appraisal. Faules concentrates upon two issues in his article: the functions of appraisal and the perceived quality of the appraisal system. Areas of convergence were found; for example, both sets of data provided evidence that the employees questioned whether there really was a connection between ratings of individuals' performance as a result of their appraisal and their actual job performance. However, divergent findings were also noted; for example, Faules found that the qualitative interviews picked up a practice that was seen as unfair by most employees, namely, when an initial appraisal by a person's boss is changed by someone else. However, this theme was not covered in the questionnaire, which only addressed issues that Faules had thought of at the outset of his research. There is clearly a thin line here between saying that the two sets of results are inconsistent and saying that the qualitative data qualify the quantitative. Also, it is easy to see in this case the suggestion that the qualitative data are more comprehensive and realistic, because the researcher has not tied his respondents to pre-determined categories in closed-ended questions. However, it could also be argued that had the researcher undertaken a pilot study comprising open-ended questions as a precursor to designing his questionnaire, as is often recommended in textbooks (for example, Schuman and Presser, 1981), the particular divergence that has been focused upon here may not have arisen.

The tendency for interviews in qualitative studies to generate more detailed and comprehensive information than in postal questionnaires and structured interviews may therefore be mitigated in part by greater preparation prior to the design of the research instruments. However, the key point that is being made is simply that the criteria for deciding whether two sets of data are inconsistent or whether one set (the qualitative) simply embellishes the other are unclear. It is not insignificant that Faules was not very specific on this issue though, in concert with the tendency described above, he does say that the qualitative element 'provided the most insight' (p.161).

The widely-supported notion of triangulation being an important rationale for integrating quantitative and qualitative research is by no means as unproblematic and uncontentious as it first appears. Some resolution of the kinds of issue described here is required before the idea can be taken much further.

The interweaving of quantitative and qualitative research

How to achieve a true interweaving — Grounded Theory

There is a tendency for most illustrations of integration to involve the use of both quantitative and qualitative research in such a way that each represents a separate block of data collection, for example, when a researcher using semi-structured interviews also administers a questionnaire. Rarely are the two interwoven so that they feed off each other in the sense of stimulating new issues for data collection, regardless of whether a quantitative or qualitative approach is employed. This is why researchers working within a triangulation mode simply draw attention to incongruence and often arbitrarily depict one set of data as representing the true picture. What they could consider is to resolve the issue by further data collection, though they may face the problem of deciding whether the extra data should be quantitative, qualitative, or both! Research which conceives of quantitative and qualitative research as relevant to different stages of an investigation (approach no. 10) is especially likely to involve a more iterative approach to their combination (e.g. Gross et al., 1971; Tharp and Gallimore, 1982).

Another context in which quantitative and qualitative research are interwoven seems to arise where the researcher is faced with a puzzle. Whyte's (1976) research on Peruvian villages demonstrates this attribute. Whyte was reading an anthropological field report on one of the villages and was surprised to find that it exhibited low levels of both conflict and cooperation. His surprise arose because there is a tendency to think of the two as polar opposites. He reconceptualized them as separate and independent continua. In order to determine whether this reconceptualization made sense in practice, he analyzed aggregate survey data that had been collected on conflict and cooperation in these villages and confirmed his hypothesis. Survey data relating to each village for each of two years (1964 and 1969) were then examined in terms of conflict and cooperation. This analysis revealed that one village had undergone a pronounced change from a combination of high cooperation and low conflict to low cooperation and high conflict. In order to understand this change better, he collected further information using an ethnographic (i.e. qualitative) approach. *Mine! Conceptual model*

Whyte describes his approach as one of 'weaving back and forth among methods' (1976, p. 216), something which happens very rarely in the cases of integration that I have come across. It is also striking that such a strategy fits well with the notion of grounded theory in which the investigator moves backwards and forwards between data collection and the elaboration of theory (Glaser and Strauss, 1967). Grounded theory is generally depicted as an approach to the analysis of qualitative data, but as Glaser and Strauss made clear, both quantitative and qualitative *Very important* methods and data can be employed in generating grounded theory (Glaser and Strauss, 1967, p. 18). Consequently, the notion that the integration of quantitative and qualitative research can take on a more iterative character, in which they are heavily interwoven, fits well with the general ethos of grounded theory, which could be regarded as providing a framework for such exercises. Of course, time and money act as constraints on the capacity of researchers to allow the data collection process to spiral in the way Whyte describes, but if we accept that integration can occur across research projects, and not just within them, then it becomes more feasible.

The approaches to integration are not always planned

It is clear that many researchers explicitly plan to employ both quantitative and qualitative research. However, it should not be presumed that the various approaches to integration that have been described represent the outcomes of planned designs. A researcher may undertake an integrated study with a particular aim in mind, but then he or she may find when the data are analyzed or even as the data are being collected that mixing methods serves a different purpose. For example, a researcher may aim to conduct an integrated study in order to capture both structure and process with a single study (integration approach no. 5 in mind) but may find that the combined data better serve the illumination of the differences between subjects' and his/her own perspectives (approach no. 6).

In itself, such a fortuitous outcome does not represent a problem and in many ways it constitutes an advantage of combining quantitative and qualitative research. In fact, researchers may seek to combine the two research styles for a host of reasons, many of which are fairly tentative.

This may mean that many of the outcomes of integrating quantitative and qualitative research referred to above are not just unplanned, but may even be post hoc reconstructions of the process of and reasons for integrating methods. This is not to say that some researchers attempt to deceive, but that we have very few guidelines for the contexts in which the two research styles can or should be combined. This makes it inevitable that some outcomes will be unanticipated. What seems to be needed is much greater thought about why research that combines quantitative and qualitative research is worth doing. If we take the view that there are no universally superior research designs or methods, and that the critical issue is the appropriateness of a design or method for the research question, the same criterion ought to apply to combined studies too. This would mean that we need to think about the circumstances in which integrated research is appropriate and what sorts of advantage might accrue.

Tactical advantages of integration

Integrated studies can facilitate the tactics of doing research. Two points stand out. First, combined research may smooth access to research sites. Faules (1982) observed that the agency in which he conducted his research was enthusiastic about the survey component but much less keen on the proposed qualitative element, though it was prepared to go along with it. Interestingly, at the report stage, members of the organization were more interested in his qualitative findings than the survey evidence, in spite of their originally lukewarm response to his proposal for this component. However, it was the survey research that helped to secure access. In other words, one might cynically suggest that it might sometimes be helpful to include a quantitative component, which is often perceived as generating 'hard' findings, in order to secure access. However, as Smith (1986) has observed, some groups may be more receptive to a qualitative than to a quantitative component. The moral here may be that an integrated approach is more likely to contain a component that will appeal to organizations to which access is sought. Again somewhat cynically, it may be that for the same reasons, proposed research which integrates the two approaches stands a better chance of being funded.

A second tactical advantage is in relation to the broad conduct of research. Marshall (1981) points to a benefit of conducting a survey by structured interview in a setting in which he had previously been a participant observer. As a participant observer in a retirement village in the USA, he had learned the times of the day when it would be inadvisable to conduct interviews because residents would be taking a nap. As he notes, a lack of knowledge in this regard could have had an adverse effect on his response rate. Also, he observes that when things went wrong with his interviewing, such as a lack of cooperation, he was able to retreat to friends and informants to help him to understand what went wrong.

Is combined research always superior?

It's the research problem that guides the decision

Much of what has been said up to now could be interpreted as implying that studies that combine quantitative and qualitative research are inherently superior to those based on a single method. This is not the case. The view taken here is that the research problem should guide the decision about whether to employ quantitative or qualitative research (and indeed which specific method of data collection should be used). Equally, this means that a research strategy that combines the two approaches is not necessarily superior in all circumstances. The researcher has to judge whether any important aspects of the research problem would be ignored if there was an exclusive reliance on one research approach.

There seems to be a growth in the number of studies combining quantitative and qualitative research and it is possible that such research will become increasingly common. It may even be the case that such investigations will come to be seen as the yardstick for good research. But we should appreciate not only that a combined strategy must be appropriate to the research problem, but also that the presence of the additional research approach (be it quantitative or qualitative) must be more than cosmetic. When properly combined, one approach enhances the other. However, if integrated research became increasingly popular, it is possible that some investigations which combine quantitative and qualitative research would be undertaken in such a way that it is difficult to detect what advantages have accrued or even what advantages the investigator anticipated. In other words, we must not get into a frame of thinking whereby research is regarded as almost by definition superior if it combines quantitative and qualitative elements. The tendency for many researchers to be trained in or inclined towards just one approach may in fact militate against the successful integration of the two research styles, even when there was a clear case for integrating them.

Integrating quantitative and qualitative research or quantitative and qualitative data?

Sometimes, researchers talk and write about combining quantitative and qualitative data rather than quantitative and qualitative research. Are they the same thing? Two points seem especially relevant here. First, data deriving from methods of data collection associated with qualitative research (for example, unstructured interviews or participant observation) are sometimes quantified, even by investigators who are wedded to the ethos of qualitative research with its distaste for 'scientific empiricism'. When the fruits of qualitative investigations are quantified, one can detect a sense of profound misgivings, for example, Crompton and Jones's (1988) discussion of their decision to code the descriptions of the work context of the white-collar employees whom they had interviewed as part of an ethnographic study of the workplace. The quantification of qualitative data is especially tempting when qualitative data are being analyzed by computer, since many programs can generate simple quantitative analyses fairly easily. The analysis of qualitative data by computer is an issue to which I will return.

Second, social survey instruments, like structured interviews and self-administered questionnaires, which are conventionally associated with quantitative research, sometimes include open-ended questions which generate qualitative data. For example, Connidis (1983a) reports the results of a study in which she collected quantitative data through a structured interview schedule concerning the preferences of older people regarding whether they preferred to live on their own or with their children. She also included an open-ended style of question that is normally associated with semi-structured interviews for qualitative research. The responses to this open-ended question forced her to modify her conclusions slightly. We may have Quant+Qual talk within one

In this study, we encounter the combination of quantitative and single qualitative data, but is this the same phenomenon as the combinations method of quantitative and qualitative research that have been encountered previously in this chapter? It differs because the quantitative and qualitative data have not been derived from different methods of data collection but from the same research instrument. The same applies to cases (such as Crompton and Jones, 1988), where quantitative and qualitative data coexist, but where the former derive from the quantification of the latter. Again, a single research instrument has been employed for the collection of both quantitative and qualitative data.

These reflections suggest a four-fold division of types of research in terms of whether the research method is quantitative or qualitative and whether the data are quantitative or qualitative. Table 2 aims to capture these distinctions.

Table 2 Linking Quantitative and Qualitative Research and Data

		Type of Method	
		Predominantly Quantitative	*Predominantly Qualitative*
Type of Data	*Predominantly Quantitative*	**1. Congruent**	**2. Incongruent** e.g. quantification of answers to semi- or unstructured interviews or observations in participant observation
	Predominantly Qualitative	**3. Incongruent** e.g. answers to open-ended questions in a structured interview schedule	**4. Congruent**

Cells 1 and 4 represent congruent types which we readily recognize as quantitative and qualitative research respectively. They are congruent in the sense that with cell 1, a quantitative research strategy generates quantitative data; with cell 4, a qualitative research strategy generates qualitative data. The combination of methods associated with these two cells is what is typically meant by the integration of quantitative and qualitative research. Cells 2 and 3 are incongruent or 'mixed' types, in which the type of data (or perhaps one should say more accurately the type of data analysis) appears at variance with the type of method employed. The incongruent cells represent combinations of quantitative

Was that combined research? (No)

and qualitative data, but in each case a single method of collecting the two sets of data has been employed. Therefore, the question arises whether cells 2 and 3 can be regarded as indicative of combinations of quantitative and qualitative research.

Although it may seem to imply a narrowness of viewpoint, there are grounds for regarding these incongruent cells as not indicative of a genuine combination of quantitative and qualitative research. Since they are not a product of the integration of the methods associated with quantitative and qualitative research, they are unlikely to reflect fully the relative strengths of these two research styles. Connidis (1983b), based on her experience of using both a structured interview schedule with some open-ended questions and a semi-structured, informal approach to interviewing elderly people, has also questioned the capacity of the open-ended questions in a structured context to generate the kinds of data that qualitative researchers typically seek. For one thing, the structured interview creates the expectation on the part of the respondent of short answers or of responses to fixed-choice questions. It is not easy for the interviewee to change gear for the more detailed kind of questioning that the open-ended question seeks. Connidis also observes that the closed-ended questions may hinder the kind of rapport that is required for genuine unstructured interviewing. Further, from the interviewer's point of view it is necessary to switch modes for the recording of answers. Nowadays, it is common for qualitative interviews to be tape-recorded, something which is unusual in the context of structured interviews. It can create an odd impression if the interviewer suddenly produces a tape recorder, having previously sought to elicit essentially brief answers, though there may be more sensitive ways of handling the switch in the style of questioning. One might also question whether open-ended questions that are tacked onto a structured schedule can really make accessible the respondent's point of view, which is the central motif of qualitative research. The semi- or unstructured interview is a tool that is employed to elicit the interviewee's categories and interpretation of phenomena that he or she regards as significant. It is a style of interviewing that is more than the sum of the parts, that is, it is more than a collection of open-ended questions and the answers thereto. Adding in a couple or even a few open-ended questions does not make for the collection of qualitative data of the kind that the advocates and practitioners of qualitative research seek. On the other hand, as Connidis (1983b) notes, the data that can emerge from the

That's why I have focus groups?

open-ended questions can help with the interpretation and understanding of broad survey findings.

What of the quantification of qualitative data from the kind of method of data collection associated with qualitative research (cell 2)? Farrant (1990), for example, describes a project in which she employed semi-structured interviews to examine the use of a water sports centre. Some of her data were coded and quantified, for example, sources of information about the centre. The section of the book in which this article appears is 'Demolishing the "Quantitative v. Qualitative" Divide'. However, it is not obvious how research of this kind can be construed in these terms, since it does not represent a convergence of the two approaches to research. Again, I am inclined to argue that cases like this do not represent examples of the integration of quantitative and qualitative research. When a qualitative researcher codes and quantifies qualitative data, the aim is generally to provide a means of summarizing a set of data. In any case, qualitative researchers often engage in 'quasi-quantification', using terms like 'many', 'most', 'often', and 'hardly ever'. In other words, the use of quantification of such data is not meant to provide the means for examining the kinds of issue that are normally of concern among quantitative researchers, such as precise calculations of relationships between variables, teasing out casual paths, providing estimates of central tendency and dispersion, inferring from sample to population and so on. Instead, quantification acts as a means of summarizing qualitative material as an alternative to a more indeterminate presentation of the data. It does not seem appropriate to regard this as an instance of the integration of quantitative and qualitative research, since it does not reflect the concerns of practitioners of the former.

One final point on this issue that is worth registering is that although it seems to me inappropriate to regard the kinds of integration that are implied by cells 2 and 3 as genuine examples of integration, they nonetheless provide helpful adjuncts to the researcher. In the case of cell 2, a helpful means of summarizing certain kinds of qualitative data (perhaps especially in connection with straightforward issues) is implied, while with cell 3, the additional data can help in the understanding of the phenomena concerned.

Is there a convergence of style between quantitative and qualitative research?

This last point is probably very speculative, but I wonder whether quantitative and qualitative research may become more similar in terms of their general approach to the enterprise of social research. The growing interest among qualitative researchers in the use of computers, which have long been the preserve of quantitative researchers, may be a factor in this regard. There is certainly evidence of a growth in interest in and use of computers for the analysis of qualitative data. A special double issue of the journal *Qualitative Sociology* (Vol. 7, nos. 1 & 2, 1984), which regularly publishes articles on the theme, recent texts by Pfaffenberger (1988) and Tesch (1990), plus a collection of chapters by a number of writers in Fielding and Lee (1991) seem to herald a new age in qualitative research.

The reasons for the growing interest in computers among qualitative researchers are fairly obvious, but four can be singled out. First, most qualitative researchers recognize that qualitative data are 'an attractive nuisance' to use Miles's (1979) phrase, since a great deal of rich data are generated, but are intractable to analysis. Second, it is also recognized that the ways in which researchers go about qualitative data analysis are very idiosyncratic in that there are few widely-agreed procedures and published qualitative research rarely makes explicit how the data were analyzed. A third factor is the growing cheapness of personal computers, and especially of machines with hard disks which are preferable for analyzing large amounts of qualitative material. Finally, and most importantly, there is a growing availability of software that aims to reflect the specific needs of qualitative researchers (Tesch, 1991). For example, a number of programs have been written in such a way as to facilitate the generation of grounded theory, such as Seidel and Clark's ETHNOGRAPH (1984), and also many programs have been devised which enable multiple categorization of text, the modification of emerging concepts, and the addition of new categories as the analysis proceeds (Pfaffenberger, 1988). These developments may have three effects that are relevant to the topic of this paper. First, it will mean that quantitative researchers will not be the only social scientists involved in the arcane discourse of megabytes, RAMs, DOSes, and hard disks. Second, I predict that the temptation to quantify chunks of data will prove irresistible (see also, Richards and Richards, 1991). Third, it will induce much greater reflection on and codification of analytic procedures, which will bring qualitative data analysis closer to the procedures associated with quantitative data analysis.

Conclusion

Quantitative and qualitative research are different, otherwise there would be no point in even discussing the possibility of combining them. They each have distinctive characteristics that make the possibility of combining them especially attractive. It is also clear each has been influenced by theoretical and epistemological concerns and issues, such as the acceptance or rejection of a natural science approach to social research, but this does not mean that they are forever tied to these concerns and issues. The view taken here is that the depiction of quantitative and qualitative research (and the alternative labels described in Table 1) as distinct epistemologies or paradigms that cannot be reconciled is both inaccurate, since they have achieved a certain degree of independence from their epistemological foundations, and unduly restrictive. On the other hand, this chapter has sought to draw attention to a number of concerns and observations regarding the combining of quantitative and qualitative research. In the end, I am convinced that awareness of the advantages of integrating quantitative and qualitative research will be so overwhelming that the doctrinaire and restrictive views of writers who deprecate the virtues and accomplishments of combined research (e.g. Smith and Heshusius, 1986) will be gradually eroded.

References

Blumstein, P. and Schwartz, P. (1983) *American Couples*. New York: Simon and Schuster.

Brewer, H. and Hunter, A. (1989) *Multimethod: A Synthesis of Styles*. Newbury Park: Sage.

Bryman, A. (1988) *Quantity and Quality in Social Research*. London: Unwin Hyman.

Bryman, A. (1992) *Charisma and Leadership in Organizations*. London: Sage.

Bryman, A., Bresnen, M., Ford, J., Beardsworth, A., and Keil, T. (1987) 'Leader orientation and organizational transcience: An investigation using Fiedler's LPC scale'. *Journal of Occupational Psychology, 60,* pp.13-19.

Bryman, A., Bresnen, M., Beardsworth, A., and Keil, T. (1988) 'Qualitative research and the study of leadership'. *Human Relations, 41,* pp.13-30.

Burrell, G. and Morgan, G. (1979) *Sociological Paradigms and Organizational Analysis.* London: Heinemann.

Campbell, D.T. and Fiske, D.W. (1959) 'Convergent and discriminant validation by the multitrait-multimethod matrix'. *Psychological Bulletin, 59,* pp.81-105.

Connidis, I. (1983a) 'Living arrangement choices of older residents: assessing quantitative results with qualitative data'. *Canadian Journal of Sociology, 8,* pp.359-375.

Connidis, I. (1983b) 'Integrating qualitative and quantitative methods in survey research on aging: an assessment'. *Qualitative Sociology, 6,* pp.334-352.

Crompton, R. and Jones, G. (1988) 'Researching white collar organizations: why sociologists should not stop doing case studies'. In A. Bryman (ed.) *Doing Research in Organizations.* London: Routledge.

Essex, M., Estroff, S., Kane, S., McLanahan, S., Robbins, J., Dresser, R., and Diamond, R. (1990) 'On Weinstein's "Patient attitudes toward mental hospitalization: a review of quantitative research"'. *Journal of Health and Social Behaviour, 21,* pp.393-396.

Evered, R. and Louis, M.R. (1981) 'Alternative perspectives in the organizational sciences: "inquiry from the inside" and "inquiry from the outside"'. *Academy of Management Review, 6,* pp.385-395.

Farrant, D. (1990) '"Seeking Susan": producing statistical information on young people's leisure'. In L. Stanley (ed.) *Feminist Praxis: Research, Theory and Epistemology.* London: Routledge.

Faules, D. (1982) 'The use of multi-methods in the organizational setting'. *Western Journal of Speech Communication, 46,* pp.150-161.

Fielding, N.G. and Lee, R. (1991) (eds) *Using Computers in Qualitative Research.* London: Sage.

Firestone, W. (1987) 'Meaning in method: The rhetoric of quantitative and qualitative research'. *Educational Researcher, 16,* pp.16-21.

Glaser, B.G. and Strauss, A.L. (1967) *The Discovery of Grounded Theory.* Chicago: Aldine.

Gross, N., Giacquinta, J.B., and Bernstein, M. (1971) *Implementing Organizational Innovations: A sociological analysis of planned educational change.* New York: Basic Books.

Guba, E.G. (1990a) 'The alternative paradigm dialog'. In E.G. Guba (ed.) *The Paradigm Dialog.* Newbury Park: Sage.

Guba, E.G. (1990b) (ed.) *The Paradigm Dialog.* Newbury Park: Sage.

Guba, E.G. and Lincoln, Y.S. (1982) 'Epistemological and methodological bases of naturalistic inquiry'. *Educational Communication and Technology Journal, 30,* pp.233-252.

Hoshmand, L.S.T. (1989) 'Alternative research paradigms: a review and teaching proposal'. *The Counseling Psychologist, 17,* pp.3-79.

Howe, K. (1988) 'Against the quantitative-qualitative incompatibility thesis or dogmas die hard'. *Educational Researcher, 17,* pp.10-136.

Jenkins, R. (1983) *Lads, Citizens and Ordinary Kids: Working Class Youth Life-Styles in Belfast.* London: Routledge and Kegan Paul.

Kahl, J.A. (1953) 'Educational and occupational aspirations of "common man" boys'. *Harvard Educational Review, 23,* 2, pp.186-203.

Kuhn, T.S. (1970) *The Structure of Scientific Revolutions,* 2nd edition. Chicago: University of Chicago Press.

Laurie, H. and Sullivan, O. (1991) 'Combining qualitative and quantitative data in the longitudinal study of household allocations'. *Sociological Review, 39,* pp.113-130.

Marshall, V.W. (1981) 'Participant observation in a multiple-methods study of a retirement community: A research narrative'. *Mid-American Review of Sociology, vol. 6,* pp.29-44.

McLaughlin, E. (1991) 'Oppositional poverty: the quantitative/qualitative divide and other dichotomies'. *Sociological Review, vol. 39,* pp.292-308.

Miles, M.B. (1979) 'Qualitative data as an attractive nuisance', *Administrative Science Quarterly, 24,* pp.590-601.

Newby, H. (1977) 'In the field: reflections on the study of Suffolk farm workers'. In C. Bell and H. Newby (eds) *Doing Sociological Research.* London: Allen and Unwin.

Pfaffenberger, B. (1988) 'Microcomputer Applications in Qualitative Research'. *Sage University Paper Series on Qualitative Research Methods, Vol. 14.* Beverly Hills, CA: Sage.

Rank, M. (1989) 'Fertility among women on welfare: incidence and determinants'. *American Sociological Review, vol. 54,* pp.296-304.

Richards, L. and Richards, T. (1991) 'The transformation of qualitative method: computational paradigms and research processes'. In N.G

Fielding and R. Lee (eds). *Using Computers in Qualitative Research*. London: Sage.

Schuman, H. and Presser, S. (1981) *Questions and Answers in Attitude Surveys*. New York: Academic Press.

Seidel, J.V. and Clark, J.A. (1984) 'The ETHNOGRAPH: a computer program for the analysis of qualitative data'. *Qualitative Sociology, 7,* pp.110-125.

Shapiro, E. (1973) 'Educational evaluation: rethinking the criteria of competence'. *School Review, 81*, pp.523-549.

Smith, J.K. and Heshusius, L. (1986) 'Closing down the conversation: the end of the quantitative-qualitative debate among educational inquirers'. *Educational Researcher,15*, pp.4-12.

Smith, M.L. (1986) 'The whole is greater: combining qualitative and quantitative approaches in evaluation studies'. In D.D. Williams (ed.) *Naturalistic Evaluation*. San Francisco: Jossey-Bass.

Stanley, L. (1990) (ed.) *Feminist Praxis: Research, Theory and Epistemology*. London: Routledge.

Tesch, R. (1990) *Qualitative Research: Analysis Types and Software Tools*. New York: Falmer.

Tesch, R. (1991) 'Software for qualitative researchers: analysis needs and program capabilities'. In N.G. Fielding and R. Lee (1991) (eds) *Using Computers in Qualitative Research*. London: Sage.

Tharp, R.G. and Gallimore, R. (1982) 'Inquiry process in program development'. *Journal of Community Psychology, 10*, pp.103-118.

Webb, E.J., Campbell, D.T., Schwartz, R.D., and Sechrest, L. (1966) *Unobtrusive Measures: Nonreactive Research in the Social Sciences*. Chicago: Rand McNally.

Weinstein, R.M. (1979) 'Patient attitudes toward mental hospitalization: a review of quantitative research'. *Journal of Health and Social Behaviour, 20*, pp.237-258.

Whyte, W.F. (1976) 'Research methods for the study of conflict and cooperation'. *American Sociologist, vol. 11*, pp.208-216.

Part II

Studies using multi-methods

4 The relationships between quantitative and qualitative approaches in social policy research

Roger Bullock, Michael Little and Spencer Millham

Dartington Social Research Unit

This chapter explores the relationship between quantitative and qualitative approaches in social policy research with particular reference to studies of children conducted by the Dartington Social Research Unit. Initially, it seems easy to distinguish research which uses a quantitative approach to analyze a problem from that which seeks to assess qualitative aspects of the situation under scrutiny. However, more discrete differences are difficult to identify because there are many areas of overlap. For example, psychologists often seek to measure face-to-face interactions while sociologists build qualitative judgements into large-scale surveys. But, although the borders between the two approaches are blurred, it is important to understand the contribution of each to particular research questions.

The relationship between quantitative and qualitative research approaches in social policy research has been explored on several dimensions from the philosophical underpinning of the social sciences to the practicalities of collecting empirical data. In this chapter, we neither support nor refute these perspectives but simply offer a different view. We shall propose that the relationship between quantitative and qualitative approaches stems from the theoretical perspectives applied to the issue. Thus, there is little benefit in seeking a definitive quantitative or qualitative approach to a particular research problem. This is because specific research methods such as an interview can have a quantitative dimension and data produced can be analyzed by a variety of methods. So, even though there are obvious contrasts between an IQ test and a case study, it is unhelpful to dwell too long on the differences at the level of method and data.

Our comments will be based on our experiences at the Dartington Social Research Unit where we have used a range of theoretical perspectives to guide different research studies. While unable to claim a successful resolution of the issue under question, we hope that our discussion will illustrate the ways in which the relationship between quantitative and qualitative approaches reflects the nature of the theory employed.

Why has the issue become pressing?

The increased interest in sciences largely reliant on qualitative approaches, such as anthropology, has led to an awareness of the wide range of possible methodologies. Structural-functionalist explanations, for example, which for many years dominated attempts to link individuals' interactions to wider social systems, frequently resulting in a broad perspective and a grand survey, are now unlikely to be viewed as adequate because of the difficulties in such an approach of distinguishing necessary from sufficient causes (Giddens 1976). Social policy researchers are increasingly aware of the value of interpretive research which has been shown to produce findings which address policy issues effectively. We have now moved on from the often held stereotype that views qualitative evidence as little more than descriptions of the views and feelings of a few unrepresentative individuals. What, then, have been the significant recent developments?

Initially, the principles underpinning the use of qualitative research approaches have become more clearly established and a broader literature is now available to help researchers fashion a design, interpret results and write up findings (for example, Woods, 1986; Measor, 1985; Harré, Clarke and De Carlo, 1985; Hammersley and Atkinson, 1983). While the philosophies of the interpretative sciences have been honed throughout this century, only recently has it been possible to apply the general principles systematically to policy issues. The growing status of and confidence in qualitative approaches also reflect the ability of researchers to produce sound theory from an interpretative approach and to develop plausible generalizations from a small number of 'case-studies' (see Burgess, 1988; Mitchell, 1983).

As a result, there has been an increase of qualitative research reports that have increasingly informed social policy, and researchers skilled in producing large scale surveys have begun to build intensive studies into their research designs. Indeed, few social policy research proposals currently seeking government or research foundation funding omit a qualitative dimension. Thus, those commissioning the research have quite rightly asked, 'What is the link between quantitative and qualitative research approaches?'

Definitions of social policy research

Before we begin to answer this question, we need to define social policy research and to identify the different types of work it comprises. Bulmer (1978) has described such research as empirical investigation which is used in the policy making process. While this is clearly different from research into social policy, the definition is still somewhat wide. Surely the majority of social researchers would hope to produce findings relevant to policy developments although, naturally, academic studies may not necessarily be read by people making policy. In addition, some research does not start life as social policy research but later becomes absorbed into that process. Moreover, academic influence on social policy arguably comes as much from general theoretical observations as from empirical investigations, especially if they achieve a currency within a sympathetic political or social climate. Consider, for example, the impact of Bowlby's (1951) separation theories on child-care policies or the relationship between Goffman's (1961) total institutions and the growth of community care. Social policy research, therefore, can be defined as that which is intended or expected to be used in the politics of change. However, it can have empirical and theoretical dimensions, each with varying degrees of relevance to the policy maker.

Social policy research also covers a range of activities each of which is different in its time and resource implications as well as its functions. In broad terms, it falls into three groups. Firstly, there is research which is theoretical and fashions concepts and combines them into perspectives; this is usually part of an academic discipline or sub-discipline. Secondly, there is large-scale empirical work which provides new information based upon reliable data. Such studies review situations and provide evidence on hypotheses. Thirdly, there are evaluations of particular situations, client needs or professional practice. These studies are usually brief and limited but can be extremely useful if placed in the context of wider knowledge. At Darlington we have at various times undertaken each of these types of research: theoretical work, for example our discussion of the concept of social control as it applies in residential institutions (Millham et al. 1981) ; large scale empirical studies, such as our scrutiny of 450 children passing through local authority care (Millham et al. 1986); and specific evaluations, such as our survey of all children who were the responsibility of a particular social services department (Millham, Bullock and Hosie, 1984).

However, experience has taught us that categorising research in this way can be somewhat artificial because each type is closely linked to the others. Large-scale empirical studies need to be guided by well-considered theories. Similarly, theoretical work which involves no data collection draws heavily upon knowledge produced by empirical studies if its conclusions are to stand. Likewise, although short-term evaluations, such as our scrutinies of individual intermediate treatment schemes for delinquents, have limited value when read alone, they are an important component of our general knowledge about services for adolescent offenders built up by theoretical and empirical work.

Although researchers may consistently seek to produce studies which are relevant to policy, the usefulness of their work as perceived by policy makers tends to reflect the type of investigations undertaken. In our experience, central government and local authorities find large-scale empirical studies and short-term evaluations particularly useful, whereas it is often claimed that theoretical work is more relevant to the interests of university departments and the research councils. Theoretical research is slow, its conclusions may not be immediately applicable and there can be many 'blind alleys', for instance the numerous psychological studies which have sought to identify deviant personality traits. Yet, such claims over-simplify the situation for in the long term much theoretical research is very significant; it contributes to the drift of ideas, it fashions concepts which ultimately influence practice and enable us to ask better questions. In practice, therefore, it is difficult retrospectively to locate the exact origin of new ideas and to decide whether or not the research that feeds them is of a theoretical or empirical kind.

It can thus be seen that any definition of social policy research must incorporate the fact that such work has several dimensions. This contributes to difficulties in understanding the possible contributions of quantitative and qualitative approaches because each type of research tends to employ different methodologies. Large-scale surveys are likely to be highly quantitative whereas one-off evaluations can be either quantitative or qualitative. How, then, can we best explore the differences between the two research approaches?

Differences between quantitative and qualitative research

Quantitative work, by definition, implies the application of a measurement or numerical approach to the nature of the issue under scrutiny as well as to the gathering and analysis of data. The methodologies adopted are likely to include extensive surveys which can consider broad issues, incorporate a range of factors, include a wide geographical spread of representative samples and a focus on group outcomes. Others have called this a macro- approach but the interchangeable use of this category with the term quantitative is misleading as it rests on the assumption which we shall question later that macro-approaches must be quantitative. Qualitative investigation, in contrast, is often viewed as an intensive or micro- perspective which relies upon case studies or evidence gleaned from individuals or particular situations but it can, as we shall see, be large scale. Like Finch (1986), we view qualitative research as an approach which explores the processes behind observed associations between factors, charts individual outcomes and explores the meanings and contexts of individuals' behaviour. Thus, quantitative and qualitative approaches differ not only in the methods employed but also in the perception of the problem and the type of data they produce.

Distinguishing between quantitative and qualitative research approaches at this abstract rather than methodological level has led us further to identify the various contributions we can expect from each to the final research product. Quantitative approaches can provide authoritative survey data and relate diverse factors. They can also assess the incidence, epidemiology and boundaries of problems of the situation under scrutiny. Within such an approach it is possible to compare areas of the country and sub-groups or sets of factors can be selected for further consideration. Such work contributes to policy development at an administrative level, such as in the framing of legislation, the planning of services or monitoring the implementation of change.

Qualitative approaches, in contrast, lead to a much greater understanding of the meaning and context of behaviours and the processes that take place within observed patterns of interrelated factors. They also reveal the different perceptions which participants have of the same situation and allow researchers to consider personal histories and developmental factors.

However, it is noticeable that few social policy studies have exclusively adopted one approach at the expense of the other. For example, the large-scale empirical studies conducted at Dartington have been based upon quantitative surveys but have been tempered by qualitative analysis. For example, *After Grace-Teeth*, a follow-up study of 1138 boys leaving eighteen approved schools, also provided information on the 'staff world' within such institutions and of the boys' perspectives on their training experiences. *Locking-up Children* charted the characteristics and traced the progress of 570 leavers from local authority secure units but considered these findings in the context of the history of security for children in England and an analysis of the regimes offered within the institutions under scrutiny. *The Chance of a Lifetime*, a study of boarding school education, was supplemented by the highly qualitative *Hothouse Society* which explored in greater detail the lives of children through their own writing, letters and poems.

More recently, we have completed another predominantly qualitative study of the lives of forty five young men passing through the prison system (Little, 1990). However, this research is best read in the context of the other largely quantitative investigations into juvenile delinquency which have preceded it and which are reviewed as an introduction to the research. Thus, it seems that studies which are methodologically partisan usually rely on or are supplemented by evidence derived from other approaches.

This mix of quantitative and qualitative approaches has its critics; indeed, Platt (1971) has described it as an 'old tradition' and others have referred disparagingly to an over-reliance on 'cross-tab and case-study' approaches. Critics despair at what seems to them to be opportunist eclecticism in which unstructured interview material dominates survey data or vice versa. But, it is our experience that eclectic approaches only fall short when eclectic means ad hoc, selected for their convenience rather than theoretical relevance. If, however, eclectic means a combination of the best features of different approaches as and when appropriate, it is our experience that a research methodology is usually strengthened. One particular perspective may, of course, still be dominant, setting the programme for conceptualizing the problem, processing the data and analyzing the results, but it will be complemented and, hopefully, illuminated by others. Four models of linking quantitative and qualitative approaches are common, all of which have been used effectively in social policy research.

The first model is where the quantitative findings are illustrated by qualitative case studies. As we have said, this has been criticised because the case studies appear to do little more than vividly illustrate the findings of macro-data. However, if developed in a more sophisticated way, case studies can be used to study processes and explore themes that occur within a general cluster of factors and can chart, explain and assess the consequences of individuals' perspectives. An examination of exceptional cases or statistical outliers can also prove illuminating.

A second way of mixing quantitative and qualitative approaches in social policy research is the use of qualitative results to explain the findings of quantitative research. For example, from studies in the 1950s it became well-known that children's educational attainments were closely related to their social class. The qualitative investigations of Bernstein (1965) explained this finding in terms of the language codes used by children from different social groups, a factor that would not have been evident from quantitative analysis of social class and children's attainments.

A third relationship is to use qualitative evidence to produce hypotheses which can be tested quantitatively. For example, detailed studies of children in care suggest that services are supply led, a hypothesis currently being explored at the University of Bristol in a much wider analysis of trends in child-care statistics. While the issue of whether more children enter care at times of economic growth is still debated, this wider argument would have been dormant without the initial micro-hypothesis.

Finally, we can identify social policy research which links methods by using qualitative studies to produce typologies which improve the understanding of factors explored through quantitative evidence. These typologies may be based upon ambiguities or disputes about social processes. For example, in our study of the links between children absent in care and their families, we sought to monitor contact between parents and offspring (Millham et al. 1989). The instruments used to measure access patterns in an extensive survey were much improved by a qualitative investigation of the informal barriers to contact experienced by families. This revealed that even in situations where social workers saw no official restrictions on access, parents and children faced enormous difficulties in maintaining links with one another.

Several other relationships between quantitative and qualitative research approaches have been suggested by Bryman (1988) and our four models are not exhaustive. However, categorising research studies neatly into the typologies proposed poses further difficulties for reasons we shall explain. Moreover, while the categories describe links between quantitative and qualitative approaches, they do not explain the relationship between them or show how a balance is achieved. To do this, several other features of social policy research have to be taken into account.

Other features of the relationship between research approaches

Initially, we have to consider the diverse historical antecedents of quantitative and qualitative approaches. The positivist tradition which underpins much social policy research is less than sympathetic to qualitative perspectives (Finch, 1986). Moreover, the interpretative social sciences, which have increased in influence, have been equally dismissive of quantitative methods. In this context, many social policy researchers have allowed their work to be dominated by one stance without fully understanding or harnessing the benefits of the other. Thus, qualitative studies are often appended on to quantitative research in a cosmetic or unnecessary way.

We must also take into account the range of disciplines which contribute to social policy research. Psychologists, sociologists, economists and historians are among the many investigators involved. Each academic discipline tends to favour some research approaches more than others but the components of quantitative and qualitative methodologies may differ in each case. For example, it is often assumed that study samples will be larger in quantitative studies than in qualitative research. Yet, psychologists often use large samples to comprehend qualitative phenomena, for example as in Cleaver's (1991) intensive survey of the problems faced by individual children transferring from primary to secondary school which focussed on 121 pupils. Conversely, many quantitative surveys undertaken by sociologists are based upon samples of less than 100.

Terminology can also be a problem. For example, an interactionist study is not, as sometimes described, a qualitative investigation of a few cases but is research into the interactions between people. As in studies of crowd behaviour, it is possible to scrutinize the interactions of several thousand people in one small qualitative study (e.g. Marsh, 1978). One of the reasons for this confusion is the inclusion of terms such as 'interactionism' in an attempt to make perfectly valid studies of small groups seem more scientific. Yet, there is no need for this; there is exemplary research based upon a handful of cases which have proved invaluable to policy makers. For instance, Kahan's (1979) study of ten children *Growing up in Care* employs a clear research approach, namely an analysis of biographical data gleaned from a series of interviews.

However, a particular problem with social policy research is engaged or concerned with the question of challengeability or refutability. The language used by qualitative researchers tends to be less defensive than that used in quantitative (statistical) research. Partly what is at stake, therefore, is the political usefulness of the two approaches. Single case studies, such as the report on the death of Jasmine Beckford (London Borough of Brent, 1985) can win hands down under certain conditions whilst 'reliable' surveys score in other settings. But, the inevitable restrictions arising from such difficulties and the limits they impose on the choice of research subjects and approaches should not, as Tizard (1990) has emphasised, be confused with the scientific handling of evidence. Qualitative approaches and the analysis of the material they produce are just as amenable to scientific rigour and objectivity as quantitative methodologies and statistical data. Indeed, Carlen's (1990) lambast of bad ethnography as 'nothing more than conversational snippets sandwiched between disjointed sociological ruminations' can be matched by equally devastating diatribes on poor quality quantitative work and the empiricism it generates.

The research process

Although we have emphasised the difficulties of linking quantitative and qualitative approaches, researchers generally succeed in overcoming these problems. This is clear if we look more closely at the process of research and examine the links between the two approaches at different stages.

If we look at our attempts to tackle this at Dartington, several stages in the research process can be identified, steps which exist whether the research is theoretical, large scale empirical or a specific evaluation.

Studies usually begin with a perception of gaps in knowledge or a customer request which can take several forms; the focus of the work can be an explanation, for example 'why do children become delinquent?', an evaluation, such as 'what is the effectiveness of custodial sentences in stopping delinquency?', or a monitoring or assessment of a situation or service. To begin with, we translate the questions posed, either by ourselves, colleagues or a research customer, into discrete, manageable issues the explanations of which will have relevance to the variety of audiences we seek to serve.

In formulating a manageable research issue, we apply middle-range theories which, as we shall see, are sets of perspectives and interrelated concepts about social situations which have been found useful in previous work. We also try to develop new frameworks as necessary, perhaps undertaking some pilot work to see how theories work in practice.

We then fashion a research design which incorporates quantitative and qualitative methods appropriate to the task in hand, the important point being that the mix of methods and the relationship between approaches reflect the theoretical work which has already taken place. These methods are subsequently applied, the evidence is then assembled and, finally, an explanation of the issues is presented. It is the middle-range theories considered that are key in this process as they not only help us to clarify the problem and develop hypotheses but they also influence the explanations we put forward. Let us look at their significance in more detail.

The use of middle-range theory

There is considerable confusion about the meaning of theory in social policy research. It can refer to wide philosophical perspectives on social structures or historical change; it can explain specific problems or illuminate particular sectors of society and sometimes can even refer to a set of research methods. Distinctions between types of theory have been proposed by several writers. For example, Jahoda (1989) describes differences between down-to-earth explanations and high-level abstractions. Empirical researchers tend to produce the former but describe their results as the latter, for example by using theories which explain persistent delinquency among adults to explain adolescent misbehaviour. Down-to-earth explanations specify particular groups, situations or contexts and encompass deviants. High-level abstractions, in contrast, aim to be comprehensive and thus generalize situations and usually ignore deviants. Yet, explanations and high-level abstractions are both described by social psychologists as theory, sometimes interchangeably.

Further clarification is provided by Merton (1957) who distinguishes between grand theory, middle-range theory and minor working hypotheses. Grand theory provides perspectives and concepts about society which cannot be tested empirically but which offer frameworks to guide research. Minor working hypotheses, in contrast, are very specific to a particular subject area; they are intended to be tested but the results have little immediate wider relevance. In between these two extremes is middle-range theory which usually derives from, and is subsequently applied to, parts of society such as complex organizations or economic sub-systems. This middle-range theory effectively links concepts and suggests working hypotheses, the results of which can further develop the original theoretical approach; developments in organization theory or labelling are examples.

How does our experience of social policy research at Dartington fit with Jahoda's and Merton's distinctions? We have generally sought not only to produce explanations of social phenomena based upon empirical investigation but also to develop more abstract observations based upon accumulated knowledge within a specific field. For example, in our recent scrutiny of difficult young people in Youth Treatment Centres, we have again found that boys are much more likely to offend after leaving the institutions than girls (Millham et al. 1989), findings which duplicate those from many similar studies which we and others have completed during the last twenty five years. This led us to re-consider explanations for the high offending rate of boys. We concluded that, in part, the contrasting roles adopted by and expected of older adolescent boys and girls was important in explaining their differing offending rates; persistent delinquency is an acceptable role for some boys. This generalization based upon accumulated empirical evidence will, in turn, lead to a better understanding of other roles as a way of explaining aspects of social behaviour.

Thus, we attempted to draw from our Youth Treatment Centre research both high-level abstractions and down-to-earth explanations of phenomena, to use Jahoda's division. Sometimes, ideas may derive from work in other subject areas, for example from other residential institutions we have studied, such as public or approved schools. Here, previously developed theory may help us understand a wider range of social problems and processes in other organizations. Although we draw different levels of theory from our work, it is usually of an intermediate nature, neither trying to explain how the world works nor being tied to the problem under scrutiny.

An illustration: Lost in Care

Having explored the type of theory used in our work, we shall illustrate how the research process led to a particular mix of quantitative and qualitative methods in one large-scale study, *Lost In Care*. Again, this is not to offer final solutions to this difficult problem but to explore options and explain our decisions in the hope that they will be illuminating. This investigation stemmed from a concern that the family links of children in care withered over time even in situations where social work plans supported their maintenance and enhancement. The perceived research need was for both an assessment of the extent and nature of the problem and an explanation as to why the family links had declined. In our formulation of the issues involved, we considered several theoretical perspectives but two seemed particularly pertinent; the first concerned 'process and career', the second, 'the relationship between formal and informal social systems'.

In successive child-care studies we have applied the idea of 'process and career'. In each, we have noted the propensity of individuals to follow particular 'career routes', in which one experience is closely tied, both culturally and statistically, to its sequelae. This feature of social life was equally true of the public school children scrutinized in *The Chance of a Lifetime* as it was of approved school boys looked at in *After Grace-Teeth* or the adults undergoing social work training, as studied in *Learning to Care*.

These career routes are not, however, fixed as new opportunities open up whilst others disappear. Our research studies have suggested that career routes reflect both the informal and formal processes within the social systems with which each individual comes into contact (Millham, Bullock and Cherrett, 1972). Formal processes are those structural patterns of norms, values and rules that prescribe an individual's behaviour and our expectations of him or her, and which are usually apparent in the laws and traditions of institutions. Informal processes are the social relationships and rules which evolve in group situations.

They can exercise functions not performed by formal processes, such as providing affective support within a prison. In some social systems formal processes dominate, in others informal processes are the most important. But all social situations reflect some interaction between the two.

In *Lost in Care*, the application of a career perspective to the initial research problem led us to view the family links of children in care in their wider context; that is in the light of the child's care history and upbringing. The value of a longitudinal view was also clear as the rapidly changing circumstances of the children and their families greatly limited the value of snapshot pictures of their family links.

Once it was agreed to view family links within the wider context of the child's care career, we sought an explanatory approach which would incorporate both the formal processes affecting links, such as social services' attempts to enhance or control family contact, and the informal processes involved, particularly the difficulties of visiting and maintaining emotional relations at a distance. We subsequently tested and developed this approach during a pilot study.

We were also concerned to develop a research design that would cover all children in care whatever their age, family circumstances or length of stay. Thus, we decided to follow up prospectively all entrants to care over a specified period, 450 in all, and, cognizant that formal and informal processes would impinge upon individual career routes, decided to employ quantitative as well as qualitative research methods and associated techniques. In explaining the separation of children in care and their withering links with parents, we were able to explore the informal processes which contribute to such a situation. Examples of these are: the welcoming or hostile attitudes of foster parents and residential staff; cultural expectations about visiting; the stigma associated with having children in care; and the difficulties for contact arising from the complex and multiple problems faced by families. Only by adopting a qualitative approach could we investigate the changing perceptions, roles and behaviours of family members following the child's admission to care and the way that definitions of the child's situation change, such as when abuse disclosures give a new light to a child's difficulties. These were both shown in the quantitative analysis to be closely related to outcome measures of parent-child contacts.

The important point of this illustration is that the balance of quantitative and qualitative approaches employed and the linking of the data they produced were largely pre-determined by the decision to use the theoretical perspectives of 'process and career' and 'the relationship between formal and informal processes' that guided the research from the outset. They were not, as Cicourel (1964) has suggested, simply a problem of method.

Limits to the application of middle-range theory

While this description of a research process has attempted to clarify how the mixing of quantitative and qualitative approaches became explicit in the final research design, three additional features of our use of middle-range theory help further clarify the relationship between the two approaches. Firstly, we only apply theoretical perspectives in a specialised field of interest and, in individual studies, to specific study groups. We avoid universal explanations of human behaviour, limiting our efforts to the explanation or monitoring of particular issues. Our perspectives may have wider relevance but our focus is specialized and specific.

Indeed, it is for this reason that we apply and generate middle-range theories. The subject area, services for children and their families, does not lend itself to universal laws. For example, whilst poverty could be used to explain the difficulties of children in care, such grand theory is not very useful given that most poor parents bring up their children without social services' help. This latter group, deviants from the grand theory, are not within our area of research.

Secondly, during the subsequent stages of any research, we also find that theories are modified and perspectives combined so that the final explanatory model is usually eclectic, in the ordered way previously described. Thus, although certain aspects of the research process are expected to go together, for example sophisticated statistical techniques to scrutinize survey data, we find that the research process is much more complicated than this and that unexpected liaisons often prove fruitful. This is particularly true of the mixture of and relationship between quantitative and qualitative methods.

Thirdly, we do not apply middle-range theory in a zealous way; we do not believe in our theory and do not assume an ideological stance. A theory is only useful in so far as it helps us to formulate, understand and explain an issue. If it does not work, we look for the reasons why it fails to apply and either adapt it or abandon it altogether.

The strengths and weaknesses of the Lost in Care approach

In describing these research experiences, we do not seek to suggest that the research process we describe is either used frequently or the best available; it is only relevant in so far as it offers another way of linking quantitative and qualitative research approaches.   Indeed, we can identify several strengths and weaknesses in this model.   Its major strength to the researcher is that it produces explanations, not just descriptions, which have relevance to both the academic debate on an issue and the research customer.

Because our work is focused on policy issues, we are also able to use theoretical perspectives which seem the best available at the time of study, given the state of knowledge within the disciplines contributing to our field. However, herein lies the weakness. Given the small number of social policy researchers, there is little competition between theoretical perspectives; indeed, it is more likely that researchers working on similar issues will produce complementary approaches or that the theories of one will be subsumed into the perspectives of others. Moreover, as middle-range theories tend to be implicit rather than clearly stated in research reports, it is difficult for commentators to criticise them, particularly in view of the lack of comparative data against which competing theories can be judged.

Nonetheless, as expertise among and liaison between researchers improve, it is hoped that the middle-range theories which guide the research process will become more sophisticated and authoritative and provide wide-ranging findings relevant to the social problems we study. Within this context, the mixture of quantitative and qualitative approaches and the relationships between them will be better understood.

Conclusion

In this chapter we have sought to explore the use of and relationship between quantitative and qualitative research approaches in social policy research and, in particular, the Dartington Social Research Unit's studies of children and families. Social policy research is an umbrella term sheltering several pursuits. A few fortunate individuals can sit in ivory towers, usually mock Gothic, fashioning theories, uncontaminated by findings or feelings. Others work tirelessly to produce new and reliable evidence to shed fresh light on long-standing social problems. The majority of social policy research is, however, short term and sharply focused upon specific client groups or problems of immediate concern to professional or political groups.

Clearly, there are contrasts between the drawn-out musing of the lofty academic and the swift, small scale investigations undertaken by those producing answers for policy makers. However, each is dependent upon the others and has differing relevance to policy makers. In the long term, however, the theoretician can also have a considerable impact upon policy, partly because of the influence of such work on the nature and type of empirical research and on the ways in which problems are perceived. All social policy research, therefore, we would argue should include a clear theoretical component.

The contributions that quantitative and qualitative research approaches can make to investigations are clear and in our own work we usually apply a combination. Based upon this experience, we have suggested several models of linking the two: 'the cross tab and case study combination'; the use of qualitative findings to explain quantitative results; using qualitative research to develop hypotheses that can be tested quantitatively and to develop typologies which can be scrutinized in a quantitative manner.

But whilst these models are useful in that they lead us to rethink our methods and to reconsider our use of quantitative and qualitative approaches, they can also be misleading. Social policy research is a complex exercise. It has different philosophical traditions, includes a range of disciplines and answers to a multiplicity of audiences. Consequently, one person's quantitative approach becomes another's qualitative study. Thus, rather than categorizing relationships between each approach, we need to begin with a theoretical formulation of the issue and then choose appropriate methods.

We can better understand the role of quantitative and qualitative approaches by improving the definitions of the terms we use, by providing clearer descriptions of the research design in research reports and by conducting investigations which are guided by clear theoretical principles. We have explored the use of theory in social policy research and find that theories that underpin our work help to conceptualize the problem under investigation, suggest the research methods we use in the study and influence the explanation that is finally offered. We have concluded that within such an approach, the use of and relationship between quantitative and qualitative approaches is implicit in the theoretical perspectives adopted.

We do not wish to suggest that this is a foolproof answer to the questions posed at the beginning of this chapter. There are several shortcomings in our approach, many of which have been identified by those who take a critical view of the way knowledge is commissioned and produced (Bell and Newby, 1977). What we have suggested is very much a research practitioner's perspective, the view of people who attempt to respond to perceived knowledge gaps, policy problems and customer requirements. As such, the theory we have discussed tends to be middle range, lying between what Merton (1957) has described as minor working hypotheses and grand theory.

Looking from the outside and taking a much broader philosophical view, it is possible to be highly critical of our stance, to characterise it as blinkered and insular and to see a collusion between contractor and contracted which dictates the selection of quantitative and qualitative methods (Weiss, 1977). Others may propose that quantitative and qualitative methods are fundamentally different, that they cannot be integrated. The nature of the evidence produced and the thought processes, whether convergent or divergent, guiding their analysis cannot be reconciled. Such criticisms are beyond the scope of this paper and we accept that, from such a position, our suggestions may appear as mere navel searching. We can only stress that we can find few social policy research studies which rely solely on a qualitative perspective and none which have not been informed by or stand alone from other quantitative investigations. It is our contention not that research should be either quantitative, qualitative or both, but that it is best guided by well-considered theory. The need for discipline and rigour applies whatever the type of social policy research, be it theoretical, large-scale empirical or specific evaluations.

References

Bell, C. and Newby, H. (1977) *Doing Sociological Research.* London: Allen and Unwin.

Bernstein, B. (1965) 'A socio-legal approach to social learning'. In J. Gould (ed.) *Social Science Survey.* Harmondsworth: Penguin.

Bowlby, J. (1951) *Maternal Care and Mental Health.* London: HMSO.

Bulmer, M. (1978) 'Social science research and policy-making in Britain'. In M. Bulmer (ed.) *Social Policy Research*. London: Macmillan.

Burgess, R.G. (ed.) (1988) *Studies in Qualitative Methodology. Volume 1: Conducting qualitative research*. London: Jai Press.

Bryman, A. (1988) *Quantity and Quality in Social Science Research*. London: Unwin/Heinemann.

Carlen, P. (1990) 'Review of Villains: Crime and community in the inner city'. *Sociology, 24*, pp.735-736.

Cicourel, A.V. (1964) *Method and Measurement in Sociology*. London: Collier-Macmillan.

Cleaver, H. (1991) *Vulnerable Children in Schools: A study of catch 'em young, a project helping 10 year olds transfer school*. Aldershot: Dartmouth.

Finch, J. (1986) *Research and Policy: The uses of qualitative methods in social and educational research*. London: Falmer.

Giddens, A. (1976) *New Rules of Sociological Method*. London: Hutchinson.

Goffman, E. (1961) *Asylums*. Harmondsworth: Penguin.

Hammersley, M. and Atkinson, P. (1983) *Ethnography: Principles in practice*. London: Tavistock.

Hammersley, M. (1990) 'What's wrong with ethnography? The myth of theoretical description'. *Sociology, 24*, pp.597-616.

Harré, R., Clarke, D. and De Carlo, N. (1985) *Motives and Mechanisms. An Introduction to the Psychology of Action*. London: Methuen.

Jahoda, M. (1989) 'Why a non-reductionist social psychology is almost too difficult to be tackled but too fascinating to be left alone'. *British Journal of Social Psychology, 28*, pp.71-78.

Kahan, B. (1979) *Growing Up in Care*. Oxford: Blackwell.

Lambert, R. and Millham, S. (1968) *The Hothouse Society: An exploration of boarding school life through the boys' and girls' own writings*. London: Weidenfeld and Nicholson.

Lambert, R., Millham, S. and Bullock, R. (1975) *A Chance in a Lifetime? A Survey of Boys' and Co-educational Boarding Schools in England and Wales*. London: Weidenfeld and Nicholson.

Little, M. (1990) *Young Men in Prison: The criminal identity explored through the rules of behaviour*. Aldershot: Dartmouth.

Marsh, P. (1978) 'Life and careers on the soccer terraces'. In R. Ingham, S. Hall, J. Clarke, P. Marsh and J. Donovan *Football Hooliganism: The wider context*. London: Inter-Action Imprint.

Measor, L. (1985) 'Interviewing in ethnographic research'. In R.G. Burgess (ed.) *Qualitative Methodology and the Study of Education.* Lewes: Falmer Press.

Merton, R.K. (1957) *Social Theory and Social Structure.* Glencoe: Free Press.

Millham, S., Bullock, R. and Cherrett, P. (1972) 'Social control in organisations'. *British Journal of Sociology, XXII*, pp.406-421.

Millham, S., Bullock, R. and Cherrett, P. (1975) *After Grace-Teeth: A comparative study of residential experience of boys in approved schools.* London: Human Context Books.

Millham, S., Bullock, R. and Hosie, K. (1980) *Learning to Care: The training of staff for residential social work with young people.* Aldershot: Gower.

Millham, S., Bullock, R., Hosie, K. and Haak, M. (1981) *Issues of Control in Residential Care.* London: HMSO.

Millham, S., Bullock, R. and Hosie, K. (1978) *Locking Up Children: Secure provision within the child-care system.* Farnborough: Saxon House.

Millham, S., Bullock, R. and Hosie, K. (1984) *Social Services for Adolescents in Croydon.* Barnardo's/Croydon Social Services Department.

Millham, S., Bullock, R. Hosie, K. and Little, M. (1989) *Access Disputes in Child-Care.* Aldershot: Gower.

Millham, S., Bullock, R., Hosie, K. and Little, M. (1989) *The Experiences and Careers of Young People Leaving the Youth Treatment Centres.* Dartington Social Research Unit.

Mitchell, J.C. (1983) 'Case and situation analysis'. *Sociological Review,* pp.187-211.

Platt, J. (1971) *Social Research in Bethnal Green: An evaluation of the work of the Institute of Community Studies.* London: Macmillan.

Tizard, B. (1990) 'Research and policy: Is there a link?' (9th Vernon-Wall Lecture) *The Psychologist,* October, pp.435-440.

Weiss, C. (1977) *Using Social Research in Policy Making.* Lexington: Lexington Books.

Woods, P. (1986) *Inside Schools: Ethnography in educational research.* London: Routledge and Kegan Paul.

5 Integrating methods in applied research in social policy: a case study of carers

Hazel Qureshi

Introduction

This chapter describes an example of social policy research in which qualitative and quantitative approaches were used simultaneously during data collection, and some measure of integration in analysis was also achieved. I am at one with Bulmer (1986), Bryman and Hammersley (this volume) among others, in arguing that there is no necessary connection between a decision about the use of qualitative or quantitative methods and a particular epistemological position, nor is a particular method of reasoning uniquely associated with one kind of approach. Bulmer, for example, describes the contrasting quantitative and qualitative paradigms in policy research, but stresses that these are ideal-typical constructions which reflect competing meta-methodological views of social science. He goes on to argue: 'when scrutinized critically neither the logical nor the methodological line between qualitative and quantitative methods is a hard and fast one'. (Bulmer, 1986, p.189)

John Seidel, the inventor of the ETHNOGRAPH programme for computer assisted analysis of qualitative data, observed that although the computer did no more than to perform much more quickly the same tasks which he had previously performed with pen, paper, cards, scissors and large amounts of floor space, nevertheless the use of the computer seemed greatly to enhance his credibility with quantitative colleagues (Seidel, 1989). 'At last qualitative analysis comes of age' seemed to be their view. As someone who has undertaken qualitative analysis by both methods I can see why this kind of response is irritating. However, it perhaps illustrates that the so called qualitative/quantitative divide is as firmly rooted in the sociology of the profession as in any basic philosophical difference between the approaches.

If this is so, perhaps it is in order for me to set out an explanation of my own background, to explain where I stand in relation to this 'divide'. My undergraduate training was in pure mathematics and philosophy, but at the end of this I turned, perhaps in reaction against an excess of abstraction, to work in statutory and voluntary social services for several years. To gain more relevant knowledge I took courses in sociology and social administration, and developed an interest in social research related to practice. I obtained a qualification in quantitative methods and subsequently secured a post in a Social Services research unit. However, the first research I was asked to undertake related to a topic which appropriately lent itself to investigation by qualitative methods, since it was focused on the motivation of volunteers and paid helpers working on an experimental community care project. From exploratory pilot work it seemed that people might not be explicitly aware of their initial motivations for undertaking this kind of voluntary or quasi-voluntary caring work, and might be helped by careful in-depth discussion and, in particular, retrospection to the point at which they first made their choice. Abrams (1978) found that some of the inferences drawn by him from open-ended discussion about motivations for undertaking voluntary work were rather unpopular when fed back to interviewees, because they were felt to reflect badly on those involved, and this strongly suggested that any checklist of possible motivations, which a structured approach might have employed, would have been highly likely to be subject to social desirability effects. For these reasons a less structured approach to data collection seemed to be appropriate, but in a research unit famed for its quantitative approach a strong case had to be made for such a departure from normal practice.

The experience of using a less structured interviewing approach convinced me of its value, because the results cast doubt on taken-for-granted assumptions in the original research design that all of the paid and unpaid helpers would be undertaking this activity because they were receiving 'rewards' of some kind. Unstructured methods made it possible to uncover unanticipated responses which led to the creation of a more adequate framework for understanding their participation (Qureshi, 1985). In subsequent work I have always employed both quantitative and qualitative methods but the different kinds of data have not been so closely linked in analysis as in the study which will be described in this chapter. My background has given me an appreciation of the strengths and weaknesses of quantitative and qualitative methods, but as an applied social researcher with a primary focus on 'problem' areas, I stand somewhat outside on-going debates about conflicting methodological paradigms within sociology. I have no 'axe to grind' for any particular methodology except in relation to a specified problem area.

The only aspect of the epistemological/methodological debate on which I would like to comment concerns apparent widespread misconceptions of the philosophy of the natural sciences. In their definitions of positivism writers in social science rarely seem to reflect currently accepted models of the natural sciences. The influential work of Popper (1972) on the logic of scientific dicovery, and of Kuhn (1962) on the practice of 'normal' science within the framework of accepted paradigms seems to be ignored in favour of a 'straw man' conception which would have little credibility within the philosophy of science. Finch (1986) for example offers the following:

> positivism is taken to mean an approach to the creation of knowledge through research which emphasises the model of the natural sciences: the scientist adopts the position of the objective researcher, who collects facts about the social world and then builds up an explanation of social life by arranging such facts in a chain of causality, in the hope that this will uncover general laws about how society works. The underlying logic is deductive, where a hypothesis is generated from a universal statement, then tested by empirical research, which then leads to a verification or a modification of such universal generalisations   (Finch, 1986, p.7).

First, it is by no means clear that the first sentence of this quote implies the same process as the second.   Second, neither of these descriptions reflects a currently accepted model of the natural sciences. Within the philosophy of science the myth of an objective scientist collecting 'facts', without a prior theoretical framework or frame of reference, is widely rejected: 'the belief that we can start with pure observation alone without anything in the nature of a theory, is absurd.' (Popper 1972, p46, quoted by Magee, 1973). It is moreover a little surprising to see social scientists writing about the 'verification' of universal generalizations, (this is a term which Strauss (1987), a key writer on qualitative analysis, also uses extensively), despite the demonstration by Popper (1972) that such a process is impossible. Instead, Popper makes a strong case that falsifiability rather than verifiability is the key characteristic of scientific statements, which may not be verified but may be regarded as supported or 'corroborated' by evidence each time they are tested and not falsified. Debate around these issues still continues but positivism as described by social scientists holds no sway within the philosophy of science, and certainly has no logical connection with the use of quantitative methods. In their practice, sociologists committed to an interpretive epistemology do not thereby reject the models associated with the natural sciences. Strauss (1987), for example, writes: 'effective social science research must follow the example of physical science research in its intertwining of the formulation of provisional hypotheses, making deductions and checking them out' (p. 14).

Glaser and Strauss (1967) argue that the inductive reasoning which underlies the creation of theories grounded in data gives these theories a superior status to other 'speculative' theories. Within the philosophy of science there are many suggested ways to judge between competing theories. For example, do they explain more than other theories, or do they explain the same phenomena more simply? What range of testable implications may be drawn from the theory? To what degree have these been tested? The origin of the theory, whether grounded in data or otherwise, has been considered less useful as a criterion. It may be that grounded theories perform better by some or all of these other criteria, but if being 'grounded in data' is in itself the criterion of a 'good' theory then the statement by Glaser and Strauss is true but tautologous, i.e. it gives us no information other than a definition. Popper (1963) argues that theory generation, whilst it may or may not involve induction as a method of reasoning, should be seen as a psychological rather than a logical process. The argument that theory generation is a creative act which may not be subject to logical analysis is compelling, although it should not be supposed that this constitutes a denial that inductive reasoning may be useful in theory generation.

What must be questioned is the idea of any essential connection between inductive reasoning and qualitative methods. Inductive inferences are frequently made in relation to quantitative data. For example, in this chapter the analysis of interviews with a group of parents caring for disabled young adults will be used as a case study in integrating qualitative and quantitative analysis. These parents all lived in a particular geographical area, and so any assumption that the results may be generalized to the open class of all parents caring at home in similar circumstances is an inductive inference with no statistical foundation (Hacking, 1976). Only quantitative data collected in particular ways permit statistical inference, but many quantitative studies, in arguing for the generalizability of their results beyond the limits of permitted statistical inference, suggest (some perhaps only implicitly) inferences which are not statistical, although they may be plausible or reasonable. These are inductive inferences in that they move from the particular to the more general.

The study reported in this chapter is a piece of 'applied research' in social policy, that is, research directed towards practical use within certain policy or problem areas, undertaken by researchers employed or contracted by policy makers. There are obvious policy and resource constraints on subject matter and methodology in this context. My focus in any piece of work is on 'the problem'. I am not particularly interested in generating 'theory', but am prepared to borrow, in an eclectic manner, from disciplines which I am competent to understand, any theories or methods which seem to cast light on the chosen problem area, or to suggest changes in policy and practice. In this chapter I will therefore try briefly to indicate the outcomes of the research study in relation to these latter aspects because that is an important part of the way in which I would wish the value of my work to be judged. Certainly a range of criteria exist for judging the worth of policy-related research, although there is no doubt that judgements about the relative merits of such research are rarely made on solely logical or methodological grounds. It is suggested that policy makers have been sceptical about the value of qualitative research in general (Finch, 1986), but there is some evidence of improvements in this situation (Walker, 1989). Certainly, Department of Health customers raised no objections to the use of qualitative elements in the research programme discussed in this chapter, which was agreed for funding in 1986 (Kiernan and Qureshi, 1986). The particular problem area under consideration was the care of people with mental handicap who showed behaviour problems. Such behaviour problems might include attacks upon other people, self-injury, the destruction of property, and a range of other socially unacceptable behaviours.

Background to the study

Of course, in an important sense, the concept of 'behaviour problem' is socially constructed in ways which reflect norms of behaviour in particular situations. Attacks upon others are judged acceptable in war, or the boxing ring; self-injury occurs, for example, in a variety of religious practices or festivals. In relation to mental handicap there were clear differences in staff tolerance of particular behaviours in hospital as opposed to community settings. These differences were reflected in the literature and in our own pilot qualitative work (Fraser et al, 1986; Kiernan and Qureshi, 1986b). Nevertheless there was a wide measure of agreement that there were people with mental handicap who showed behaviour that was sufficiently challenging to services to mean that additional resources were required for their care. It was also generally accepted that, in the past, the usual service response to such individuals, certainly once they reached adulthood, was to place them in long-stay hospitals.

Many 'interested' groups can be identified in relation to the politics and practice of deinstitutionalization of people with mental handicap (Hardy et al, 1990). These include: medical, nursing and other staff of long-stay hospitals; Local Authorities and their staff who provide community services; parents and other advocates for people with mental handicap; and the disabled individuals themselves (not to mention policy makers who are concerned about restraining public expenditure). People who showed behaviour problems were a pivotal group in relation to debates about this topic in 1986 because the capacity of community services to care for them in adulthood was not well-demonstrated, and the need to provide suitable care for them was being used as an argument for the retention of specialist hospital units and medical expertise in the face of demands for care in the community. There was also a climate of concern about parents as carers, and the extent to which they could reasonably be expected to take on the continuing care of their adult sons or daughters at home if the alternative of hospital care were no longer available. The Department of Health was interested in assessing the numbers and current location of people in this particular group and thus they commissioned the Hester Adrian Research Centre to carry out a broad epidemiological survey in a range of Health Districts in the North West of England. This large-scale survey provided an opportunity to conduct a linked study of parents providing informal care. It was decided that whenever an adult aged eighteen to twenty-six and living in their parental home was identified in the epidemiological study, an interview would be sought with the parent responsible for his or her care at home. This interview was designed to investigate the following: the experience of caring at home for a young adult with mental handicap and behaviour problems, the costs to parents, their evaluation of the services they received, and factors influencing an expressed preference for alternatives to family care. It was in relation to this latter study of parents, mostly mothers, that the use of both qualitative and quantitative methods was attempted, for a range of reasons which will be outlined.

Ninety-two per cent of parents were approached and, although in most areas we were not able to follow up people who did not reply to an initial letter, full interviews were obtained in seventy per cent of instances. We were able to use data from the wider survey to compare respondents with non-respondents. Age, sex, level of intellectual functioning and severity of behaviour problems were compared for the young people whose parents were, and were not, interviewed and no significant differences emerged. Although there are no statistical grounds for generalizing the results beyond the seven Health Districts concerned, there is no particular reason to suppose that services for people with mental handicap are markedly different in other parts of the country, though the North Western Regional Health Authority area has a reputation for a relatively enlightened approach to services (Audit Commission, 1989; NWRHA, 1985). The Health Districts were chosen to include Districts representative of all types found in the Region in accordance with a cluster analysis based on their socio-economic characteristics (Craig, 1985). However, despite these arguments for wider representativeness, any generalization beyond the Districts concerned is an inductive and not a statistical inference.

Considerations affecting choices between qualitative and quantitative approaches

Much of the available evidence suggests that the presence of behaviour problems in the cared for person is a factor which causes psychological distress in carers (Quine and Pahl, 1985; Sloper et al, 1991) and also makes it more likely that relatives will seek alternatives to family care (Wilkin, 1979; Grant, 1988). Thus we are dealing with primary kin relationships in situations which are known to be highly stressful and possibly prone to breakdown. In considering how the research should be undertaken, it was clear that the subject matter of an interview with parents would probably be highly sensitive and could be potentially distressing. Too structured an approach might damage rapport as well as being upsetting for parents. On the other hand, the methods used in the wider epidemiological study were of necessity quantitative, and obviously this larger study provided considerable, potentially comparative information, both about the wider context within which the young people living at home received their services, and about the ways in which the young people concerned were seen by staff.

The fact that these particular parents were the carers of a targeted sub-group of the individuals who were identified within the comprehensive epidemiological survey, meant that there were strong grounds for considering them to be a representative group of family carers (at least in the Health Districts in question). This had the consequence that quantitative data could be useful to service agencies in these Districts in relation to planning and evaluation. However this way of finding the parents also meant that the identification of the young people as being members of our target group had been carried out by staff in service facilities, not by their families. This was important because although it had been decided to seek interviews with all apparently relevant families, in the event local agencies placed some restrictions on who could be approached in a small number of cases. Agencies refused access, for example, where a family member had recently died, and, perhaps less reasonably, in a few cases where they felt that parents would react badly to the identification of their child as showing behaviour problems. This potential for conflict over definition brings us back to the point mentioned earlier about the ultimately social nature of the definition of the term 'behaviour problems'. It was necessary to be able to be flexible in our approach to parents, and in the conduct and structure of the interview, because parents might well reject the whole idea that their child showed behaviour problems. In fact two parents approached did reject the idea outright, arguing that any problems which occurred in services were a reflection upon service providers and their failure to understand the young person's behaviour. An inflexible interview schedule, predicated upon an assumption that the parents would acknowledge the existence of behaviour problems, would have been quite inappropriate in such instances.

Thus the research strategy in this study was influenced by a number of considerations which pointed in different directions. The sensitive content of the material to be covered and the social nature of the definition of the phenomenon under study suggested that qualitative methods would be desirable. On the other hand, the representative nature of the group, the existence of comparative data available from the wider survey, and the interest of service agencies in using results for planning and evaluation of their services, indicated the need for quantitative methods. It was decided to attempt to collect from parents in one interview a core of basic information using structured questions, but also to include in the interview substantial unstructured sections for open-ended discussion of selected issues (Ritchie and Sykes, 1986).

The research interview

All interviews were tape-recorded and the interviewers were full members of the research team, employed on academic-related pay scales, in recognition of the fact that qualitative interviewing requires substantive knowledge of the area as well as technical skills. A qualitative interview is an exhausting process for the interviewer, involving the necessity to listen, process information, and plan the next stages of the interview simultaneously. The interviewer needs a clear knowledge of the purpose of the interview, the practical and theoretical concerns of the research, and the context which influences the respondents' replies. In this sense a good qualitative interview is nothing like a 'normal conversation', except perhaps that it has a superficial resemblence to the kind of conversation in which a person might tell their life story to a stranger on a train. The interviewers received intensive training in techniques of unstructured interviewing. The content of the training was based on a course attended by the author at SCPR, extended by the use of video feedback on role-playing interviews, and discussion of the aims and context of the particular research. The team listened to and discussed taped pilot interviews conducted by the author.

The aim in the parent study was to collect qualitative and quantitative data within the same interview. (See also Bryman in Chapter 3, and Brannen's work described in Chapter 1). Clearly this can pose difficulties since it may be thought that too structured an approach will inhibit the free expression of feeling or the expression of unanticipated responses or, on the other hand, that the completion of pre-coded questions will be too difficult if the respondent is allowed to be too discursive. Most of the questions in the interview were asked in an open-ended way, even where there were precoded categories already established for recording the answers. The only exceptions were the questions on household income and a few specific evaluative ratings of services where showcards were used. Pre-coded categories of answer were established in advance if it was felt that existing knowledge from the literature and previous research made it possible to construct these categories in ways which we were confident would represent accurately the respondents' likely range of answers. For example, there is considerable work on costs borne by parents, including financial costs (Baldwin, 1985) and a range of other social, emotional and health costs (Carr 1985; Byrne and Cunningham, 1985). Of course there was a risk that answers given to questions asked in an open-ended way in a particular interview would not fit the anticipated categories. If this occurred then interviewers did not impose the given categories but explored the unanticipated response in detail, and this part of the interview was transcribed from the tape for further analysis. This helped us to keep a check on the degree to which the categories we were using were adequate to reflect the answers given.

In those areas of questioning where it was felt that there was insufficient prior understanding of likely responses, the interviewers used an interview guide consisting of topic headings and suggested questions (Lofland, 1971). For example, unstructured techniques were used in discussing parents' perceptions of the causes of problem behaviour because existing understanding of this area was very limited. For different reasons open-ended discussion was also employed when discussing parents' thoughts about the future care of their son or daughter. Although there was some excellent prior qualitative work to build on (Richardson and Ritchie, 1986), the sensitivity of the area required a flexible and non-directive approach in the interview. Finally, some areas of investigation lent themselves to the collection of both kinds of data. In relation to the evaluation of services, for example, it seemed important to have a precise idea of how much use was actually made of services, and to collect some structured evaluative data along dimensions such as reliability, sufficiency and suitability, which had been used in other evaluative studies (Challis and Davies, 1986; Grant, McGrath and Humphries, 1987). However, it was also possible, by introducing open-ended discussion about services or professionals whom parents had found particularly helpful, or unhelpful, to uncover the dimensions which parents themselves used in making judgements about services. At the end of the interview, the main carer was asked to complete two structured pen-and-paper scales: the Judson self-rating scale (Judson and Burden, 1980) and the Malaise Inventory (Rutter,

Tizard and Whitmore, 1970). These scales provide useful comparative data because they have been widely used in studies of parents, particularly mothers, and they reflect parental adjustment to handicap and levels of psychological distress. Interviewers could vary the structure of the interview as appropriate and had flexibility to switch out of sections which were clearly not working in individual cases, or to abandon a particular line of questioning. This ensured that, for example, where a person was excluded from services, the interviewer could spend time discussing the perceived reasons for, and feelings about, such exclusion rather than trying to collect evaluative ratings of services which were no longer used. Although there was this flexibility in the use of the schedule in the field, the content of the interview schedule could not evolve or change as the collection of data progressed because the time-scale allowed for completion of fieldwork was not sufficient to allow any detailed qualitative analysis to begin whilst interviews were still in progress. In addition, since it was hoped to make comparisons with data recently collected from staff in services, the time gap between collection of data from different sources needed to be kept as short as possible. Even with a time gap kept to a minimum, one young person had already moved from home into residential care by the time her mother was interviewed. This latter interview gave valuable insights into the factors surrounding one particular admission, but could not be included in quantitative analysis relating to, for example, Malaise Inventory scores, because psychological distress could no longer be assumed to be associated with the presence of the young person in the home.

In summary, within the overall interview structure, factors underlying a decision to use a less structured approach were: little available existing knowledge; the potentially sensitive or distressing nature of the particular topic; a wish to focus on the parents' own constructions of a particular concept. A structured approach was used when there was detailed relevant knowledge available from previous research, and where there was a desire for data which would be explicitly comparable across cases, and with other studies, and with other sources of data which were available within the overall programme of work on behaviour problems. Structured questions also made clear the exact levels of service being received, for example, in terms of hours per week of day care being used by the young adults. I would argue that the proper atmosphere for open-ended discussion can be maintained if there is sound prior information on which to base the questions and the expected range of answers, so that they seem natural to the respondent even when structured, and do not seem to require a distortion of his or her experience.

Linking qualitative and quantitave data

Processing the different kinds of data

Structured sections of the interview were coded and processed so that the data from them could be added to the existing SIR database which already held the information from the large-scale epidemiological study. SIR was used because of its capacity to handle hierarchical data, and to generate SPSS system files, at various levels of the hierarchy, which could subsequently be used for complex statistical analysis (Robinson et al, 1980). Our files were hierarchical because they contained information about service settings, staff assessments of individuals and, in some instances, parents' views.

All open-ended sections of the interviews were transcribed, together with relevant comments made during other sections, and disagreements with existing precodings. The selection of relevant sections was carried out by the interviewers who, in some cases, where the recording was less clear, dictated them onto a second tape for ease of transcription. Tape counter references to the original interview tape were entered in the transcripts, so that tracing back to the original section of the recording was possible. This exercise was time-consuming and costly. Between four and six hours of work were necessary to achieve a transcription of one hour of interview. Transcriptions were entered directly into a micro-computer using a word processor (WordPerfect), and were subsequently coded by embedding codes in the text before and after the appropriate sections. This was carried out by the author. The four main areas of interest in the parent interview provided the first level of coding, or division into categories, for the depth analysis framework (Ritchie, 1987). These were: parents' experiences of living with and responding to behaviour problems, perceived costs to parents, their views of services, their views about future care for the young person. Within each of these initial four categories, a tree structure of further coded categories was developed from expectations derived from the literature and preliminary readings of the transcripts. Space does not permit a full elaboration of the final complete index of coded categories. Of primary interest here is the analysis of parents' expressed attitudes towards the idea of the young person living away from home in future because, as will be outlined, this was the main area of qualitative analysis from which the emergent categories were systematically linked to the quantitative data.

Linking during analysis

Computer-assisted analysis of the coded transcripts was undertaken using a program (SEARCH) developed by David Reeves, the Hester Adrian Research Centre statistician, in collaboration with the author. This program essentially performed the task of grouping and referencing quotes with similar codes, but it also had the capacity to restrict analysis to specified, ordered subsets of the transcripts. It was possible to use SPSS to generate lists of transcripts according to criteria related to quantitative data. These lists were then used as input into the SEARCH program. For example, groups of marginal or deviant cases, where observed statistical relationships did not hold, could be selected and their interview transcripts subsequently searched for relevant codes. The listing of referenced quotes generated by this search constituted output for further analysis. If necessary this output document could be recoded and searched again, thus refining any initial categories identified. Alternatively SPSS could be used to order the transcripts before searching. For example, when considering qualitative data on parents' views of services, it was useful to have extracts from transcripts labelled and grouped in order of Districts, so that it was possible to take some account of variations in the service context across Districts. Equally, it was possible, for example, to compare single mothers with married mothers, or people whose children were excluded from services with those who were not. In this way quantitative data from the structured precoded questions was used in the selection and ordering of qualitative data during analysis.

Where a categorization of parents was constructed using qualitative data this could be added to the SIR database as a new variable, and subsequently used in suitable quantitative analysis. Of course, caution needs to be exercised in performing such a transformation, which may be thought to divorce the categorization from its grounded meaning. Seidel (1991) argues that such uses of 'coded' categorized data carry the risk of reification, that is, of making an unwarranted assumption that these are somehow pre-existing categories waiting to be counted rather than being an artefact of the relationship between researcher and data. The variable which has been used in this way in this chapter is a categorical variable reflecting parents' expressed attitudes towards the future care of their son or daughter. There is no doubt that the quantitative variable used is a crude oversimplification of the complex range of reactions and feelings expressed by parents. However, because the details of the emergence of these categories through qualitative analysis are known, we do have access to these complexities and confusions and are thereby able to set a more meaningful context for the discussion of quantitative results. The following sections will consider in more detail the ways in which existing quantitative data influenced the process of qualitative analysis, and in which qualitative data were used to cast light on the failure to find an expected statistical relationship.

Categorising parents' responses about their children's future care

A community-based study by Grant (1988) had found that around half of parents of adults with mental handicap were oriented towards continuing home and family care in the foreseeable future. In the current study only eight out of fifty-nine parents interviewed expressed such an orientation and this was often as much a rejection of statutory services as an enthusiasm for family care. A recurrent theme across the majority of interviews was an extreme reluctance on the part of parents to see their other children's lives affected by caring in the same way that their own had been. 'I don't want the burden to fall on my other two children. It's affected our lives to look after him and I don't want them going through the same thing', said one mother, who was hoping that statutory care would be available. Another mother, who did not feel that residential services would be suitable for her son, saw only one satisfactory solution to the problem of the long-term future: 'I'm really hoping that he goes before me in a way ... I don't know ... I don't really want (his sister) to ruin her life with him.'

Three-quarters of all parents saw non-family care being required at some point in the future, and one in three expressed views which implied that this was needed immediately or in the near future. Parents were not classified as wanting alternative care immediately unless they had already made positive efforts to secure a long-term residential placement for their son or daughter. Parents who wanted such care for their sons or daughters 'soon' were distinguished from those who felt it would be required 'eventually' because they indicated a range of factors which suggested that family care could not continue for long, even though this was frequently coupled with assertions that they wanted to continue as long as possible and, in some cases, with signs of considerable distress at the thought of not being able to continue.

> We don't like thinking about it now. 'Cos we know ourselves that we've got to give it up when we can't manage it ... If we could stay where we are now, we'd all be happy, but we can't. She's getting heavier. I mean, I can hardly lift her up. (Mother)

> It's me now that needs some help to cope with him, or to be able to pay somebody to look after him ... There will come a day when I can't ... I should be retired ... There will come a time when I won't be able to do it. (Mother, single parent)

A number of cross-cutting themes emerged from the analysis of views about the future. One of the most prominent in relation to choices about the future was the widespread perception that there were no suitable long-term residential services available in the community for young people with mental handicap who showed problem behaviour.

> There just isn't anywhere, 'cause if you have a child with behaviour problems, or profoundly handicapped, you're at the back of the list every time. (Mother)

> I wouldn't want her to go into (hospital). No way, it's too institutionalized, I'd hate it. We would like a small ... like she is here at home, exactly the same ... every time you talk to them you get the same thing: 'There's no money'. (Mother)

These comments suggest that attitudes towards the future do not in most cases represent a positive choice by parents, but rather an acceptance of the inevitability of the eventual necessity of non-family care reached in a situation of considerable uncertainty about the likely availability of acceptable services in the future.

> I remember saying to L. (Community Nurse), 'What would happen if we dropped dead, where would he go?' And she said 'Well, really I just don't know.' So if she doesn't know, well I certainly don't. That was when he was being quite a problem. I suppose we just live from day-to-day hoping a place will come about. (Mother)

Even among parents who wished to carry on caring for the foreseeable future, there was a desire to commence some kind of planning for the long term, together with services, so that the eventual transition could be phased in gently, while parents were still alive and able to participate in their child's care. For these parents, the current policy concern with developing practice which will 'preserve' or 'maintain' informal networks (Griffiths, 1988; Cm 849, 1989) misses the need to plan for and implement the transfer of caring responsibilities which is considered to be at some point inevitable in the majority of instances.

The analysis described in the previous section gave rise to the following categorization of parents' views in relation to future care:

	No.	%
1. Avoids subject/doesn't want to think about it	3	5
2. Hopes for independent living for young person	4	7
3. Hopes for continuing family care	8	4
4. Non-family alternative needed eventually	23	39
5. Non-family alternative needed soon	14	24
6. Non-family alternative wanted now	6	10
7. Other	1	2
	59	100

In terms of quantitative analysis, interest centred on the twenty people who were identified as considering giving up care now or in the near future (groups 5 and 6). A quantitative variable was constructed which reflected whether people did, or did not, belong to this group and quantitative analysis focused on finding factors associated with this.

The quantitative analysis using the variable constructed from qualitative analysis

One hypothesis, that the expressed wish for alternative care immediately or soon would be associated with high levels of psychological distress in mothers, was not supported by the data. The correlation between these two variables was very weak at .01 and indicated that they were not associated in any substantive way. Rather, psychological distress was associated with the health of the carer and with the unremitting continuous nature of the task of caring, reflected in additional domestic work, frequency of night-time disturbance and the total number of behaviour problems displayed by the young person. Consistent with this was the fact that high levels of day care were associated with lower levels of distress in mothers. In contrast, a requirement for alternatives to family care was related to the mother's perceived opportunity costs reflected in lost opportunities for employment and restrictions on social activities. It was also related to the uncooperativeness of the cared for person and the type of behaviour problems shown: severe self-injury being apparently particularly difficult for parents to cope with. The expressed wish for alternative care was not related to the level of day care received but was strongly related to the quantity of respite care received in the past year, the more respite care the more likely the wish for permanent alternative care.

These results are consistent with those from a range of other studies and have important service implications which are fully developed in other work (Qureshi, 1990a and forthcoming). Briefly they suggest, for example, that certain forms of service provision, for example, day care, may have an important role to play in relieving carer distress, but may not have any effects on carers' wish for alternatives to their own care, unless they are delivered in sufficiently flexible ways to enable carers to make good their perceived opportunity costs. They also suggest that some of the factors underlying a wish to give up may be rather intractable, so that it has to be accepted that an alternative to family care may be a necessary solution in some instances.

Qualitative analysis of cases where the initially 'expected' relationship did not occur

The finding that psychological distress and a wish for alternative care were not related was unexpected. It was possible to select out the cases where the relationship was not in the expected direction for a further exploration of the interview transcripts. There were twelve cases where distress scores were high but the mother wanted to carry on caring, and eight cases where distress scores were low but giving up was being contemplated. The most conspicuous difference was social class - those who were planning to give up but experienced relatively low distress were overwhelmingly middle class, while most of those who were going to carry on despite considerable distress were working class. Analysis of transcripts in the former cases revealed explicit evidence of planning for the future separation (mostly without cooperation from statutory services). This was often coupled with a justification in terms of the normality of the young person developing independence from their family, or the rationality, in relation to the carers' advancing age, of planning alternative care arrangements.

> I intend as I get too old to look after them, to move out of the house and leave them in a home with helpers, and the house to Mencap, you know. (Mother of son and daughter with handicap)

In contrast, most of the latter group were aware that the long-term future was uncertain, but currently their considerations about the future were inconclusive, and their aspirations (even when they themselves recognized them as unrealistic) were for a continuation of family or home care.

> Maybe he could live somewhere like that if nobody wanted him. I hope I'm not here to see it. I'd rather his own family have him. (Mother of young man excluded from services)

In one sense these class differences 'explain' the lack of a relationship between psychological distress and attitudes towards alternatives to family care. In general, working class carers had higher distress scores, which may, of course, be related to factors other than caring (see Quine and Pahl, 1985). However, they were less likely to be seeking alternatives to family care. This does have implications for decisions taken at policy level. For example, a decision to target intensive home-based assistance on situations where the young person is considered to be 'on the margin of need for institutional care', would be likely to discriminate against working class carers under high stress, who may not be expressing a wish for alternative services, and therefore are less likely to be members of the group targeted for additional services.

Qualitative analysis involving a hypothesis

The analysis of qualitative data was approached with a hypothesis in mind about attributions of intentionality and their relationship to acceptance of the person with handicap, and expressed willingness to continue caring. Specifically, drawing on the literature about coping with disorder in families, (see Orford, 1987), I anticipated that people would be more likely to wish to give up caring if they believed that unacceptable behaviour was under the conscious control of the young person. As the analysis of the data produced by unstructured questioning about causality progressed, it became clear that most parents made attributions which implied that the problem behaviour was largely outside the control of the young person. Whilst not universal, the perception that difficult behaviour, especially when at its worst, was not deliberate, was so widespread that it became clear that this would not be very useful as a quantitative variable, because its powers of discrimination within the group of parents would be very limited. The wider epidemiological study demonstrated that half of young adults with behaviour problems were already living away from their family home in community residential facilities or long-stay hospital. Perhaps it was therefore to be expected that parents who had 'survived' as carers into their child's adult years were likely to have beliefs about cause which have been demonstrated to be associated with successful coping.

However a connection, which I had not anticipated, between ideas about causality and parents' negative reactions to much professional advice on handling behaviour problems, became clear when unstructured discussions on this latter topic were analyzed. Very few parents (13%) felt that they had received any useful advice on how to handle behaviour problems at home. When parents recounted their reasons for finding the advice of certain professionals unsatisfactory, a clear connection to ideas about capacity to control behaviour emerged.

> My husband and I are still somehow convinced that it's something to do with hormones, chemicals, call it what you will, something inside of him that he has no more control over than I would say, PMT, or something like that ... nobody's really been able to talk us out of it, you know. The doctor does not always agree with us, but that's how we feel. I instinctively feel that, and that's not a cover up, I really do, that's really how we see it. (Mother)

The final sentence of this quote reflects conflicts with professionals, reported by this mother, over beliefs about the causes of the young person's behaviour. It became clear that beliefs about causality and the associated beliefs about capacity of the young person to control the behaviour, lay at the heart of difficulties which some parents had in relating to solutions suggested by professionals who wanted to urge the use of behavioural methods, or who implied in other ways, or seemed to parents to imply, that the young person could or should have control over their behaviour.

> I got the impression she was one of the new breed of psychologist and everybody was responsible for their own actions ... She seemed to think that a lot of what Euan does was entirely deliberate and that ... I don't know ... I just couldn't agree with that one hundred per cent ... some of it may be ... but not all of it.

Again this has important implications for practice. It becomes clear that in many cases certain apparent attributions by professionals cut so radically across beliefs which are central to parents' ways of coping that they cannot possibly be accepted without the risk of damage to the caring relationship (see Qureshi, 1990a and b).

Conclusion

This chapter has presented a case study in policy research, where qualitative and quantitative techniques were mixed in data collection and in analysis, albeit in relatively simple ways. In relation to the particular problem area under consideration, the care of young people with learning difficulties and behaviour problems, there were a number of conflicting influences on the choice of an appropriate methodology. The problem area itself was socially defined and therefore might be differently constructed by different actors, and its more severe manifestations were known to be likely to be distressing to those involved. This suggested that there would be value in a qualitative approach. Against this, the representativeness of the group of parents identified, the interest of service agencies in using the results and the availability of considerable amounts of comparative data were all reasons for a quantitative approach. In deciding to attempt to collect both structured and unstructured data in the same interview some compromises had to be made and, it is argued, some advantages accrued. A disadvantage from the point of view of qualitative analysis was that flexible development of the interview schedule during fieldwork was not possible. On the other hand, the flexibility with which interviewers were expected to use the schedule in the field, and the open-ended style used in asking even the pre-coded questions probably meant higher levels of missing data than might have been obtained with closed questions. The combination of methods provided important benefits. For example, I would question whether an interpretivist approach based only on qualitative data would have uncovered the association between carers' perceived opportunity costs and the expressed wish for alternatives to family care, because few carers explicitly acknowledged such a connection to exist. Given the essential role which the perception of oneself as altruistic has been demonstrated to play in relation to women's self identity (Gilligan, 1982), it seems unlikely that a justification for giving up will be explicitly couched in ways which reflect that the carer feels that her losses are too great. Nonetheless, quantitative analysis suggests that this is an influential factor in relation to the wish for alternative care. However the categorization of attitudes towards future care might not have been achieved without the use of qualitative methods, for the reasons already outlined, and a purely quantitative approach would not have given such a detailed understanding of the context of decision making and the degree to which in many cases parents decisions did not really represent positive choices among alternatives. Also qualitative analysis was essential to the discovery of important linkages between parents' reactions to professional advice about controlling behaviour and their beliefs about the underlying causes of the behaviour.

There was some integration in analysis as well as in data collection. A qualitative categorization was developed and a modified version of this was subsequently used as a quantitative variable in statistical analysis. Despite some general reservations about such a process it is argued that, used with care, it can produce illuminating results, which may at the least suggest further questions to ask of the qualitative data. A return to qualitative data after examination of the results of quantitative analysis helped to illuminate why an 'expected' statistical relationship was not present. Finally, quantitative data influenced the process of qualitative analysis by making it easier to select, order and group transcripts before either searching them for emergent categories, or extracting quotes already identified and coded as representing particular categories.

These linkages were greatly facilitated by the fact that both kinds of data were held on computer. Although all my previous research has involved collecting both qualitative and quantitative data, this was my first experience of undertaking the analysis of qualitative data using a computer. In this study the analysis and the processes of linkage were relatively simple but I have become convinced that scope for considerable progress in linking qualitative and quantitative data must lie in the computer-assisted analysis of transcripts, and the development of software to link in relevant quantitative data, in ways which will facilitate both kinds of analysis (see Fielding and Lee, 1991). Such programs do not take the 'thinking' out of qualitative analysis. If we have to accept that induction is a psychological rather than a logical process, at least this brings the comfort that computers, as yet, are not able to undertake it. In discussing the application of computer technology to qualitative data analysis, Seidel (1991) warns against forms of methodological and analytic madness which might result from allowing computer technology to drive rather than serve research. Taking due note of these warnings, I would argue that computers will, and should, play a much greater role in future in facilitating analysis of qualitative data, and that users will find their approaches to analysis altered in some perhaps unexpected ways as this particular technical revolution progresses.

References

Abrams, P. (1978) Evaluating soft findings from non-experiments: some problems of measuring informal social care. Paper presented to PSSC/PSSRU conference on Evaluating Interventions for the Elderly, June. Version edited by Martin Bulmer published in 1984 in *Research, Policy and Planning 2*, 2, pp.1-8.

Audit Commission (1989) Developing Community Care for Adults with a Mental Handicap. *Occasional Paper No. 9*, October.

Baldwin, S. (1985) *The Costs of Caring: Families with Disabled Children*. London: Routledge and Kegan Paul.

Bulmer, M. (1986) *Social Science and Social Policy*. London: Allen and Unwin.

Byrne, E.A. and Cunningham, C.C. (1985) 'The Effects of Mentally Handicapped Children on Families - a conceptual review'. *Journal of Child Psychology and Psychiatry, 26*, 6, pp.847 - 864.

Carr, J. (1985) 'The effect on the family of a severely mentally handicapped child'. In A. Clarke, A. Clarke and J.Berg (eds) *Mental Deficiency: The changing outlook*. London: Methuen.

Challis, D. and Davies, B. (1986) *Case Management and Community Care*. Aldershot: Gower.

Cm 849 (1989) *Caring for People.* Government White Paper on Community Care. London: HMSO.

Craig, J. (1985) *A 1981 Socio-economic Classification of Local and Health Authorities of Great Britain.* OPCS studies on medical and population subjects No. 48. London: HMSO.

Fielding, N. and Lee, R. (1991) (eds) *Using Computers in Qualitative Research.* London: Sage.

Finch, J. (1986) *Research and Policy: The Uses of Qualitative Methods in Social and Educational Research.* Lewes: Falmer Press.

Fraser, W., Leudar, I., Gray, J. and Campbell, I. (1986) 'Psychiatric and behaviour disturbances in mental handicap'. *Journal of Mental Deficiency Research, 30,* pp.49-57.

Gilligan, C. (1982) *In a Different Voice: Psychological theory and women's development.* Cambridge, Mass.: Harvard University Press.

Glaser, B. and Strauss, A.L. (1967) *The Discovery of Grounded Theory: Strategies for qualitative research.* Chicago: Aldine.

Grant, G., McGrath, M. and Humphries, S. (1987) 'Tailoring respite care services for carers of mentally handicapped people'. In J. Twigg (ed.) *Evaluating support to informal carers.* Papers presented at a Conference held in York.

Grant, G. (1988) *Letting Go: Tracing reasons for the different attitudes of informal carers towards the future care of people with mental handicap.* Paper presented at the 8th International Congress of IASSMD, Dublin.

Griffiths, R. (1988) *Community Care: Agenda For action.* London: HMSO.

Hacking, I. (1976) *Logic of Statistical Inference.* Cambridge: Cambridge University Press.

Hardy, B., Wistow, G. and Rhodes, R. (1990) 'Policy networks and the implementation of community care policy for people with mental handicaps'. *Journal of Social Policy, 19,* 2, pp.141-168.

Judson, S.L. and Burden, R.L. (1980) 'Towards a tailored measure of parental attitudes'. *Child Care, Health and Development, 6,* pp.47-55.

Kuhn, T.S. (1962) *The Structure of Scientific Revolutions.* Chicago: University of Chicago Press

Kiernan, C. and Qureshi, H. (1986a) *A Survey of the prevalence and characteristics of individuals with mental handicap and severe behaviour problems.* Research proposal to DHSS. Hester Adrian Research Centre, University of Manchester.

Kiernan, C. and Qureshi, H. (1986b) *Feasibility Study for a Study of the Prevalence and Characteristics of People with Mental Handicap and Severe Behaviour Problems.* Report to DHSS. Hester Adrian Research Centre, University of Manchester.

Lofland, J. (1971) *Analyzing Social Settings.* Wandsworth: Belmont.

Magee, B. (1973) *Popper.* London: Fontana/Collins.

NWRHA (1985) *Services for People who are Mentally Handicapped. A Model District Service. Services for People with Additional Special Needs.* North Western Regional Health Authority, Manchester.

Orford, J. (1987) *Coping with Disorder in the Family.* London: Croom Helm.

Popper, K. (1963) *Conjectures and Refutations: growth of scientific knowledge.* New York: Basic Books.

Popper, K. (1972) *The Logic of Scientific Discovery.* London: Hutchinson.

Quine, L. and Pahl, J. (1985) 'Examining the causes of stress in families with severely mentally handicapped children'. *British Journal of Social Work, 51,* pp.510-517.

Qureshi, H. (1985) 'Exchange theory and helpers on the Kent Community Care Project'. *Research Policy and Planning, 3,* 1, pp.1-9.

Qureshi, H. (1990a) *Parents caring for Young Adults with Mental Handicap and Behaviour Problems.* Report to Department of Health, Hester Adrian Research Centre, University of Manchester.

Qureshi, H. (1990b) 'Challenging behaviour in young adults: The parents' point of view'. *Nursing Times 86,* 45, November 7th.

Qureshi, H. (forthcoming) 'Will reducing Psychological Distress in Carers Help to Sustain Informal Care?' Hester Adrian Research Centre Working Paper, University of Manchester.

Richardson, A. and Ritchie, J. (1986) *Making the Break: Parents' Views about Adults with a Mental Handicap Leaving the Parental Home.* King Edward's Hospital Fund for London.

Ritchie, J. (1987) *Training Course in Unstructured Interviewing: Session on Analysis.* Social and Community Planning Research, London.

Ritchie, J. and Sykes, W. (1986) (eds) *Advanced Workshop in Applied Qualitative Research.* Social and Community Planning Research, London.

Robinson, B., Anderson, G., Cohen, G., Gazdzik, W., Karpel, L., Miller, A. and Stein, J. (1980) *SIR Users Manual - Version 2.* SIR, a division of ISI, Illinois, USA.

Rutter, M., Tizard, J. and Whitmore, K. (1970) *Education, Health and Behaviour.* London: Longman.

Seidel, J. (1989) ETHNOGRAPH Workshop at Conference in Qualitative Knowledge and Computing, University of Surrey, July.

Seidel, J.(1991) 'Method and madness in the application of computer technology to Qualitative data analysis'. In N. Fielding and R. Lee (eds) *Using Computers in Qualitative Research.* London: Sage.

Sloper, P., Knussen, C., Turner, S. and Cunningham, C. (1991) 'Factors related to stress and satisfaction with life in families of children with Down's syndrome'. *Journal of Child Psychology and Psychiatry, 32,* 4, pp.655-676.

SPSS - Statistical Package for the Social Sciences, SPSS Inc., Chicago.

Strauss, A.L. (1987) *Qualitative Analysis for Social Scientists.* Cambridge: Cambridge University Press.

Walker, R. (1989) 'We would like to know why: Qualitative research and the policy maker'. *Research Policy and Planning, 7,* 2, pp.15-21.

Wilkin, D. (1979) *Caring for the Mentally Handicapped Child.* London: Croom Helm.

6 Combining quantitative and qualitative methods: a case study of the implementation of the Open College policy

Margaret Bird

Introduction

Until quite recently, researchers have lived in a divided world. One camp looks suspiciously over the fence at the other and shakes its collective head at the follies it sees. Those favouring quantitative methods are fond of recounting the story of medieval schoolmen who debated endlessly the question of how many teeth there were in a horse's mouth but none would deign to do the necessary practical research to find an answer. Similarly, those wedded to qualitative methods are dismissive of what they see as mindless empiricism where, metaphorically, the tail wags the dog. Like mods and rockers, or trads and moderns, the two camps prefer purity to possible contamination by association with the other. This chapter sets out to show how in the case of some research on an important educational issue that this divide was not only unnecessary but detrimental to the chances of arriving at an understanding of key questions, such as why a policy is more effectively implemented in one situation than another. This task is attempted from the point of view of someone carrying out research within an institution. I argue that there are certain advantages in being an insider, especially one who adopts an eclectic and open attitude to differing research methods.

The main purpose of the research in question was to try to determine what factors made for the successful implementation of educational policy. The means by which this was to be ascertained was a case study -

one which set out to judge the effectiveness of a policy which was designed to promote opportunities for adults to return to education. The institution concerned was the Open College of South London, which came into being in 1983 as a quasi-federation of three adult education institutes (AEIs), four colleges of further education (FE) and a polytechnic. Each institution retained its autonomy and jurisdiction in its particular field of provision but agreed to cooperate with other institutions to improve provision for adult returners. The aim was to break down the barriers between the different sectors of education and to make post-school education more relevant to people in the locality, particularly those who had benefited least from the educational system, namely women and those from working-class and ethnic minority groups.

The Open College of South London [1] would meet the criteria for what Goldthorpe et al (1968) lay down as a case study. If opportunities for adults were going to be dramatically increased anywhere in the early 1980s, it could be argued that this was most likely in a Labour-controlled Local Education Authority (LEA) in an inner city where there was a high level of social and educational deprivation. The research was then a case study [2] concerned with the process of implementing a policy, though of course the development of the Open College had to be seen in the social, political and economic context of London in the 1980s.

To understand the methodological issues, it is important to appreciate something of my role as a research officer within the Inner London Education Authority (ILEA). The first phase of the study - an evaluation of the introductory courses in new technology in the Open College - arose as part of my normal routine work within the ILEA Research and Statistics Branch. Although the study was not, initially, undertaken with an academic purpose in mind, subsequently the study developed (for the purposes of a PhD thesis) into an investigation of the origins of the Open College initiative as well as the processes of policy implementation. My role, however, as an 'insider', albeit in a branch that was viewed as somewhat detached from the politics of County Hall, obviously influenced the research process and the methods employed.

Another fact which is perhaps significant to note is my former training and experience in research. Having undertaken a MSc in Social Research (University of Surrey) and written a dissertation employing both social systems and social action theory, my theoretical viewpoint and frames of reference undoubtedly influenced the research. Also worth noting was my commitment and interest in the subject. I had personal experience of being an adult returner to education and realised the far-reaching impact which such an experience can have. In addition, I had conducted a national survey of the subject and was aware of the results of subsequent research in the field. This knowledge and experience provided a frame of reference for the first phase of the study - the initial survey of adult returners.

A variety of methods was employed - questionnaires, in-depth interviews, participant observation and the analysis of documents. The data were both qualitative and quantitative; the research tested hypotheses and employed analytic induction to develop hypotheses. The dominance of one method or the other varied in the different phases through which the research passed. Two phases of the research can be distinguished. The first phase was a questionnaire survey of adult returners taking courses in new technology, producing quantitative data. The second phase was to interview, in-depth, three groups of people: the policy makers (politicians and officers); the central staff of the Open College; and the principals and coordinators in the institutions. These interviews provided qualitative data. Insights which resulted from the role of researcher as an 'insider' were important throughout (and are discussed below in connection with each phase of the research.) To answer adequately the research question - what makes for the effective implementation of an educational policy? - the quantitative and qualitative data had to be used interactively.

It is worth considering the reasons for adopting this combination of particular methods. In the first place, how did the methods relate to the underlying logic of the inquiry? Were, in fact, the qualitative and quantitative data used in discrete ways, either to test hypotheses or to aid in the formulation of them? Second, were there practical or political considerations which necessitated compromises in the methods selected? [3] Third, was the fact that I was a participant observer and an 'insider' influential in the outcome of the study?

My aim here is to suggest that often research can be most fruitful when both the major research methods - the quantitative and the qualitative - are utilized. In describing how the research was not restricted to any one research tradition, I also hope to convey something of the dialectical nature of the process involved which did not conform to the classic, linear (quantitative) model found in many methodology textbooks.

Phase I: The quantitative study - the evaluation of introductory courses in new technology

The logic of the inquiry (Phase I)

The raison d'etre of the first phase of the study was to investigate the high drop-out rate among adults on introductory courses in new technology. It was mainly to provide information for those responsible for implementing a LEA's policy. The first phase of the study was, therefore, a straightforward evaluation.[4] Having earlier undertaken a national survey of adults returning to education (Killeen and Bird, 1981) and being aware of the results of other studies, I could speculate about the reasons for drop out and this knowledge informed the questions asked in the survey. In part, therefore, the study was testing certain hypotheses.

Practical and political considerations (Phase I)

It was critical that the method adopted could meet the requirement for a swift response to the problem of achieving a higher rate of course completions. It also had to be manageable within the workload of the ILEA Research and Statistics Branch, where the study was just one of a number to be undertaken within a relatively short period of time. Studies that extended beyond a year were rare; decision makers wanted speedy answers to questions about the effectiveness of various initiatives. To aid in this process, the branch was equipped with a mainframe computer, programmers and statisticians. Research and Statistics also prided itself on its fast turn around of data and an ability to provide answers to questions posed by senior officers and political members.

The focus of the study also had political import; the ILEA had a high profile in the capital in relation to equal opportunities. It was important, therefore, to be able to produce quantitative data which would enable one to speak with confidence about the proportion of students taking courses who were drawn from educationally disadvantaged groups.

Given all this, it was almost unthinkable that the research design would not take the form of a survey. The officers and members of the Authority would not have been satisfied with an in-depth qualitative study of a small number of students. To ensure reliability, the sample of students surveyed needed to be representative of the different types of institution and the various courses on offer. This necessitated carrying out a questionnaire survey of a representation sample of students, as an interview study would not have been feasible given the time and resources available.

In addition, the information sought needed to be presented in a quantifiable format. First and foremost, it was necessary to establish a profile of the student population. Second, it was important to be able to say how successful the courses were in their recruitment and retention of students and in their promotion of students to higher level courses. The information was obtained, therefore, by using a highly structured questionnaire, based on one employed in a national survey of the early 1980s of mature students' participation in education (Woodley et al, 1987). The replication of the earlier study allowed for the testing of hypotheses about adult returners as well as providing a national basis for comparing the ILEA findings. Given the timing envisaged and the technology available, the research results were designed to be suitable for processing by computer.

The institutional demands in this particular example created the position of what can be called the 'hired hand' researcher (Roth, 1970). Such people will usually have been recruited because they have expertise in either the quantitative or the qualitative approach and, perhaps naturally, they tend to restrict themselves to that with which they are most confident and competent. So, even where there is no absolute commitment to a particular research paradigm, there is less flexibility than is perhaps desirable. There is no disguising the fact that, in the first phase of the research, I was in the position of the 'hired hand'.

The 'insider' as participant observer (Phase I)

Following a pilot study, it was necessary to modify the research strategy in two important ways. One came about as a result of the discovery that some course tutors were not particularly interested in the research. A lack of interest would almost certainly have led to a low response rate through poor administration of the questionnaires, making the survey unrepresentative of the opinions of the student population. Therefore I decided to collect the data myself and hence set about administering the questionnaires in situ to all the classes. This undertaking had far-reaching consequences in that it meant that I became in effect an observer in all the institutions in which students were surveyed. Had I not had a very personal interest in the subject of adults returning to education, I would not have undertaken to do this.

Secondly, as a result of the trial run, I realised that I had to obtain data on the tutors' perceptions of the Open College. Knowing that I would not have time within my busy work schedule to conduct face-to-face interviews, but assured by my initial contacts in the field that I would obtain the tutor's cooperation, I designed a questionnaire for tutors in which the questions were largely open-ended. This too was administered by me.

In processing the quantitative data I found great differences between courses in the composition of the student population, course completions, and progression routes. This finding did not surprise me because of my experience of collecting the data in the institutions and meeting with the students and their tutors. I became aware that some tutors did not know that the course which they were tutoring was advertised as an 'Open College' course. Overall, there appeared to be a wide variation among tutors in their awareness and understanding of the idea of an Open College. In part, the differences in perception were related to the contrasting cultures of two types of institution (FE colleges and AEIs). But there were also differences observed between staff within the same institution. I was reminded of other evaluations which I had conducted over a period of time in which the outcomes of the policy did not match with the policy-maker's intentions.

Summary (Phase I)

The survey of students was designed primarily to produce information for the purposes of evaluation and entailed the testing of some hypotheses about adult returners. However, as a result of being a participant observer and an 'insider' within the organization, the survey also provided the basis for formulating a working hypothesis about the process of implementing educational policy.

Phase II: The qualitative interview study of the policy makers and the policy implementers

The logic of the inquiry (Phase II)

The second and most substantive phase of the research was concerned with the origins of the LEA's policy in relation to the Open College and, most particularly, with the process of implementation. It was clear that in a case study I needed a longitudinal design which would trace the original objectives of the policy and the means by which change was effected within the organization. Previous studies (Elmore, 1982) suggested that one could either start the investigation with the policy-makers and map the process forwards or, alternatively, as I had done, begin by evaluating policy outcomes and map backwards. The weakness of the former approach is that it is based on the assumption that policy makers can control the process of implementation in organizations. On the other hand, the disadvantage of backward mapping in this case was that my observations when conducting the evaluation had led me to speculate that differences in outcomes between courses were indeed the result of problems at the centre. That is, there was much to suggest that such differences were in some way connected with the different modus operandi of the central coordinators within the various institutions which made up the Open College and who were responsible for designated areas of course development. Another and distinct possibility was that such differences arose from the differing levels of commitment of the principals and course coordinators within the FE colleges and AEIs. I therefore wanted to delay approaching these people until I had a better understanding of the origins and objectives of the policy, as seen from the point of view of political members and senior officers.

After consideration, I decided that there would need to be three stages in this second phase of the study: the first would involve interviews with senior officers and leading political members who were involved in decisions regarding the setting up of an Open College; the second would entail interviews with the former Director of Studies for the Open College and the four central administrative staff; and the third would seek interviews with the principals and course coordinators in the member institutions.

The decision to employ face-to-face interviews rather than questionnaires in the second phase arose mainly from the decision to use concepts drawn from different theoretical perspectives. It seemed to me that systems theory in harness with social action theory could inform the questions which needed to be addressed. The concepts which derive from these perspectives and, in particular, those from social action theory could not have been effectively operationalized and addressed other than by employing in-depth interviews.

System theory emphasises the objective aspects of the organization - its formal structure, goals and defined roles. It accepts the organization's definition of its own goals. Among the questions which the theory raises in relation to policy implementation are: What are the main inputs in terms of resources? How does an organization secure the involvement and compliance of its members? What are the measurable outputs? And what influence has the economic and social environment on the policy outcome? This approach is useful in mapping the policy process and in identifying some of the possible key persons in the organization.[5] I used these concepts to inform the questions I asked of the participants.

I also required a method which would enable me to explore the participants' understanding of their situation. Social action theory could be helpful here, particularly its thesis that individuals and groups form and re-affirm their goals and values in social relations.[6] This perspective offered some clue to the significance and possible meaning of the very different perceptions of the Open College development which were held by staff in the various member institutions, which I had observed while I was collecting the data on the evaluation study. Among the concepts which I sensed might be useful were: 'definition of the situation', 'culture' and 'negotiated order'. It became more and more clear that if I were to work within the spirit of this perspective the most appropriate method would be to employ an in-depth interview, using an outline interview guide and a tape recorder. To have employed a questionnaire would have been much too constraining. I needed to be able to probe and to explore the issues, as and when they arose, in the course of the interview. Information, therefore, which at an earlier stage of the study might not have appeared significant, might become so, as the respondents' answers furnished new information and insights. An interview would provide the opportunity to follow the unforeseen directions towards which, it was hoped, the respondents' knowledge might lead.

The logic of inquiry adopted during this second phase of the research therefore conformed more to the analytic-inductive model, a term coined by Znaniecki (1934) and which is outlined as a sequence of procedures by Bryman (1988, p.82). That is to say, my research strategy was a modified version of the scientific linear model of research. It involved, first, a rough definition of the problem which was seen to arise from the role of professionals in institutions. Next came a hypothetical explanation of the problem which was, in part, drawn from a review of the various literatures.[7] But even more so it derived from the first phase of the research in which I had been a participant observer. At each successive stage of the in-depth qualitative interviews with the three important groups (mentioned above), the working hypotheses were refined as more information became available and my understanding of the process of implementing policy developed. A brief description of this process is given below.

In the first set of interviews with the senior officers and the political members, I employed the working hypotheses that successful implementation of the policy would require commitment from those involved, sufficient capacity (in terms of financial and other resources) and good communications between the parties. I was exploring these hypotheses in my in-depth interviews with people but, also, identifying other factors which might be crucial in the successful implementation of a policy. From the interviews it did appear that commitment, communication and capacity were evident. However, what I also noted were the reservations which people expressed about the structure and the financing of the Open College. The research strategy therefore enabled me simultaneously to test and develop the hypotheses further. Thus I could approach the next stage better informed and sensitized to the issues.

In the second set of interviews with the central staff of the Open College, the interview material did not disprove the hypotheses, although there were evident differences in the effectiveness of the four central coordinators in developing their designated fields. It became apparent that a factor absent from my hypotheses was very important. A key problem for the central coordinators was that they had no control over the role of the other coordinators within the member institutions and therefore had to rely on their 'negotiating' skills. In addition, they were not helped by the fact that relations within the management group were fraught by the clash of cultures between further and adult education.

Again, in the third set of interviews (with the principals and course coordinators in the member institutions), I was in a position to refine the hypotheses. It was clear that I needed to have some specific information from all the institutions in order to make comparisons between them and test the hypotheses. My interviews were more focused because I also knew so much more about the nature and functioning of the Open College. Successful establishment of Open College courses, I speculated, would be most likely where resources were made available, where key people (notably the principal of the college or institute and the Open College's coordinator) were committed to the enterprise, where the culture of the institution was receptive to support from outside and where, finally, there were effective avenues of communication between people both within and between institutions.

Practical and political considerations (Phase II)

The research method in this phase was not constrained by political considerations. I was only hampered by practical limitations such as the requirement to fit the in-depth interviews into what was always a very demanding work schedule. Consequently the order in which I carried out the interviews did not follow the tidy sequence I had originally envisaged. In the event this proved to be a positive rather than a negative factor because the movement back and forth between the different levels of the organization provided contrasting conditions for the testing of the hypotheses.

The 'insider' as participant observer (Phase II)

What influence did the fact that I was a participant observer in the organization have on the research strategy adopted? Obtaining access to organizations can sometimes constitute a problem for researchers. As a research officer with a responsibility for the evaluation of the new technology courses in the Open College, I did not have a problem in this respect. I only had to discuss my proposal with the deputy director of the research branch.

Once access has been arranged researchers usually have to seek the agreement of the particular persons to be interviewed. I am certain that the 100 per cent response rate resulted from the fact that I was a research officer within the branch. There was only one senior officer whom I initially felt hesitant to approach, mainly because of a previous disagreement with him. I need not have worried. He cooperated and proved most helpful in providing policy documents and suggesting other key people whom I should approach who had been involved in the development of the Open College. As my 'net' widened, I found myself approaching people who had once held key positions in ILEA but who had since left the organization - the former Chief Education Officer, the Deputy Education Officer, the former Director of Post-Schools Branch. The overall high response rate was achieved, in part, because I was seeking to interview professional colleagues. I had, therefore, flexibility in making the practical arrangements; sooner or later I would manage to fix a date in the diary of even the busiest of people!

As an 'insider' I was used to seeing senior officers and leading members in formal committees, business meetings, management meetings within institutions and even in the dining room at County Hall. Who people lunched with, in some instances, would indicate their close colleagues and help explain a shared viewpoint. When I came to interview people, I was not relying solely on what they were explicitly saying. I was constantly interpreting what was being said in the light of all the behaviour I had observed over a period of time. As Dean and Whyte (McCall and Simmons, 1969) note, we cannot take what people say as the whole truth of the matter. As an 'insider' over four to five years of the study's duration, I was party to countless discussions with colleagues concerned with a range of educational policies. I also had a unique opportunity to establish rapport and empathy.

As an 'insider' I was also able to obtain access to the management meetings of the Open College where I was able to observe the interactions, alliances and conflicts which were evident between the representatives of the AEIs and the FE colleges. Over a period of some two years I observed how the attitudes of the participants were affected by what was happening on the wider political front. The Great Education Reform Bill (1988) was to have far reaching consequences for the whole Education Authority. Once the demise of ILEA was evident the representatives of further and adult education became less antagonistic to one another and more concerned to protect the facilities which they had developed for adult returners.

Summary (Phase II)

In Phase II, I was both testing an hypothesis about the factors which make for successful implementation of policy but also refining it as my understanding developed. Initially, I anticipated from my reading of the literature, that factors such as communication, commitment and capacity were likely to be important. After, analyzing the data from the second group of in-depth interviews, it was evident that 'control' was another important factor in the implementation of change. By the time I reached the third set of interviews, I could be quite specific about the factors which would promote the successful development of courses for adult returners. Over an extended period in the second phase of the study the research paradigm was both inductive and deductive.

Linking the qualitative and the quantitative data

Finally, I reached the point where I had developed an appreciation of the difficulties that beset the Open College development. I had viewed it through the eyes of different groups of people - the officers and political members, the central staff and the principals and coordinators in the member institutions. In addition I had collected detailed data on the development of the courses in the field of new technology which were available from the survey. Data on a number of other courses (Access, Return to Learning and Open Learning) which had been established as a result of the Open College initiative were also assembled. I needed to bring together these quantitative data, the data from the qualitative in-depth interviews and my observations as an 'insider' in order to test the hypotheses about the factors which promote the successful implementation of educational policy in institutions.

The Open College was aimed at the groups who had benefited least from the educational system - the working class, women and ethnic minority groups. Its success could be measured in terms of the number of new courses which could attract and retain adults who met the recruitment criteria. There were four central staff in the Open College each responsible for the promotion of courses in a particular field which would attract adults to return to education. From the insights gained from the in-depth interviews with the four central coordinators together with the accounts of the coordinators in the institutions I could predict that more course development would take place in the field of Return to Learning and Access provision for the targeted groups than in the other areas. This expectation was based on the knowledge that there were certain pre-conditions for successful course development and my face-to-face interviews and observations within institutions had established that these factors (discussed above) were more in evidence in two course areas than in the other two. Most noticeably, the central coordinators who were most effective were better communicators - they had established supportive networks of staff in the member institutions to promote the development of the curricula for adult returners.

I assembled the statistical information from the Open College prospectus and tested the hypothesis that the development of courses suitable for the needs of adult returners would be most likely where key people within the member institutions were committed to the idea, where the resources in terms of people's time and expertise were made available and where there was good communication between the coordinators in the institution and the central staff of the Open College. It was not simply a case of comparing the number of courses in each designated area of development, I also needed to draw on the knowledge I had as an 'insider' and that which derived from interviews with key people. Whilst, therefore, it appeared that introductory courses in New Technology were a growth area I knew from having conducted my survey in situ that there were great variations between institutions in what was being provided and the extent to which the courses catered to the special needs of adult returners. In some instances institutions had simply designated existing courses as Open College provision in order that they obtain wider publicity for courses in their institution. To test the validity of the quantitative data I needed to examine the qualitative data.

Analysis therefore involved bringing together the two sets of data. The working hypotheses had been developed and refined during the course of the research. I had identified that 'control' was an important factor in bringing about change in course presentation within institutions. From my interviews with central coordinators it was evident that all four had in effect no control over the staff in the member institutions. However, it materialised that the coordinators for Access and Return to Learning courses were able to compensate for their lack of control by being effective communicators and negotiators and the establishment of a collegial method of working with staff in member institutions.

The quantitative and the qualitative data were used in the analysis both to test existing hypotheses and to generate new ones. For example, it appeared that the factors identified as promoting successful implementation interacted with one another. Two of the four central coordinators, recognizing that they were constrained by their lack of resources from the Authority, sought further finance by acting as consultants, whilst the central coordinator for New Technology obtained substantial resources from the Department of Education and Science to purchase and equip a mobile technology unit, in the form of a converted double-decker bus. However, this individual was thus committed to serving a large catchment area (Greater London) and consequently failed to develop the particular type of courses needed by the area served by the Open College. In contrast, the central coordinators for Access and Return to Learning used their additional resources in a pump-priming way within the Open College network to promote the sort of courses needed for adult returners.

Interacting with the data, focusing at different levels, feeding back to the participants my understanding of the situation and testing it against their own I was able to establish that the conditions for effective implementation required: capacity in terms of resources (both human and material); the commitment of key individuals, the coordinators and principals of institutions; and good communication between all those concerned. The ideal conditions did not exist, but there were instances, most notably where Access and Return to Learning course areas were concerned, where there were sufficient conditions. It was these course areas which were developed most successfully by the Open College.

Conclusion

The most important factor in influencing the research method would appear to be the purpose of the research. Much of the literature associates quantitative data with the hypothetico-deductive and qualitative data with the analytic-inductive methods. The two phases of my research might appear, at first, to correspond to this dichotomy. However, a closer examination reveals that in this case, as in so many other instances of research on social policy, the two logics go hand in hand.

Phase I was primarily hypothetico-deductive, employing a highly structured questionnaire and producing data treated quantitatively. Phase II, on the other hand, was primarily analytic-inductive, employing an in-depth interview and producing data analyzed qualitatively. However, what is revealed when the research process is examined more closely is that whilst the first phase served the researcher's original purpose of providing information for the purpose of evaluation and in testing a number of hypotheses (about adult returners), it also provided the basis for the initial formulation of an hypothesis (concerning the implementation of educational policy). In the second phase, whilst the research was more exploratory than the first, it was also a two-fold process so that even within one interview, as understanding developed, hypotheses were being generated as well as tested. Also, whilst the data were treated qualitatively, they were also treated quantitatively in that I was interested in the measure of commitment, the extent of communication and amount of the resources available. Finally, the two sets of data were used interactively to test the hypotheses refined over the course of the research. Any amount of quantitative data on the number of courses under the auspices of the Open College would not have revealed anything at all about the factors which promote successful implementation of policy but, equally, without the quantitative data on the number of courses developed in the four designated areas, I would have had to rely on participants' assertions as to what courses were successful and which were not. The purpose and nature of the research therefore necessitated an eclectic approach in assembling data from a number of sources.

There are practical and political concerns to take into account which lead to compromises in the choice of method. It was clear, in this study, that the choice of method was much more constrained in the first phase than the second because of the requirement to produce data quickly and in a form which could be used by decision makers. But even where there are no apparent constraints, researchers still have to select a method and a sample that are manageable within a certain time scale. These compromises need to be taken into account when undertaking the analysis and in drawing conclusions.

Another factor influencing decisions concerning research methods is who conducts the research. What is the researcher's role in relation to the organization? More importantly, is she/he an employee of the organization? Whilst the 'outsider' might be seen to have greater objectivity and also neutrality in terms of being free of shared interests, the 'insider' has all the advantages provided by participant observation. And, if the 'insider' is able to employ an external frame of reference, partiality can be avoided and objectivity obtained. As an 'insider', I was able to establish a rapport with those whom I researched. I was also able during discussion with colleagues to test out my ideas about the processes of policy implementation. I was, therefore, well-placed to employ both quantitative and qualitative methods as appropriate to each phase of the research. Moreover, it was the interaction of the data sets, drawing on deductive and inductive logics of inquiry which proved so fruitful to the outcome of the study. The use of both quantitative and qualitative methods is to be recommended if they serve the overall purpose of the study and make research more rigorous.

Notes

1.   The Open College of South London (OCSL) was the first of four 'Open Colleges' established in London in the mid 1980s. For ease of reading the OCSL will be referred to hereinafter as the Open College.

2.   Yin (1989, p.23) provides a useful definition of a case study. See also Bernadette Robinson 'Doing Case Studies in Educational Research' (Robinson, 1990).

3.   Hammersley in Hammersley and Atkinson (1983) refers to the 'trade-offs' in which researchers are engaged in making research manageable within the resources available.

4.   Evaluation can be defined broadly as the collection and use of information to make decisions about an educational programme (Cronbach, 1987).

5.   The systems approach was employed in an earlier study of policy formulation in the ILEA by Howell and Brown (1983).   They employed the Easton (1965) model of decision making.

6.   The work of Silverman (1970) is helpful here.

7.   There were three main literatures: first the body of literature relating to policy making in LEAs; second, that concerned with the implementation of policy; third, there is the wide-ranging literature concerning organizations generally.

8.   Cooley terms this process 'sympathetic introspection'.   See Hammersley (1989).

References

Bird, M. (1985), *A Study of a Community Education Project.   Part I; Organisation and Structure*, (RS 932/85), ILEA, London.
Bird, M. (1987), *The Open College of South London*, (RS 1137/87), ILEA, London.
Bryman, A. (1988), *Quantity and Quality in Social Research*, London: Unwin Hyman.
Cronbach, L. (1987), 'Issues in Planning Evaluation' in R. Murphy and H. Torrance (eds), *Evaluating Education: Issues and Methods*, London: Harper and Row.
Easton, D.A. (1965) *A Systems Analysis of Political Life*, New York, London: Wiley.
Elmore, R.F. (1982), 'Backward Mapping: Implementation Research and Policy Decisions' in W. Williams, (ed.) *Studying Implementation. Methodological and Adminstrative Issues*, New Jersey: Chatham.

Goldthorpe, J., Lockwood, D., Bechofer, F. and Platt, J. (1968), *The Affluent Worker*, Cambridge: Cambridge University Press.

Hammersley, M. and Atkinson, P. (1983) *Ethnography: Principles and Practice*, London: Tavistock.

Hammersley, M. (1989) *The Dilemma of the Qualitative Method: Herbert Blumer and the Chicago Tradition.* London: Routledge and Kegan Paul.

Howell, D.A. and Brown, R. (1983), *Educational Policy-Making: An Analysis*, London: Heinemann.

Killeen, J. and Bird, M. (1981), *Education and Work*, NIACE, Leicester.

Macdonald, B. (1980), 'Evaluation and the Control of Education' in R. Murphy and H. Torrance (eds), *Evaluating Education: issues and Methods*, London: Harper and Row.

McCall, G. and Simmons, J. (1969) *Issues in Participant Observation: A Text-Reader.* USA: Addison Wesley.

Robinson, B. (1990) 'Doing Case Studies in Educational Research'. *Easter School Booklet E811 Educational Evaluation*, The Open University.

Roth, J. (1970) 'Hired hand research' in N.K. Denzin (ed.) *Sociological Methods: A Sourcebook*, London: Butterworth.

Silverman, D. (1970), *The Theory of Organisations*, London: Heineman.

Silverman, D. (1985), *Qualitative Methodology and Sociology*, Aldershot: Gower.

Woodley, A., Wagner, L., Slowey, M., Hamilton, M. and Fulton, O. (1987), *Choosing to Learn*, Society of Research into Higher Education, Milton Keynes: Open University Press.

Yin, R.K. (1989) *Case Study Research: Design and Methods*, Applied Social Research Methods series, Vol.5. London: Sage.

Znaniecki, F. (1934), *The Method of Sociology*, New York: Farrar and Rinehart.

7 Multiple methods in the study of household resource allocation

Heather Laurie

Introduction

This chapter reports on a project recently carried out by the ESRC Research Centre on Micro-Social Change in Britain based at the University of Essex. The Household Allocative Systems Project formed part of the preliminary work of the British Household Panel Study (BHPS), a ten year panel survey being conducted by the Research Centre which will enter the field in September 1991. The Household Allocative Systems Project explicitly used a combination of research methodologies, techniques and theoretical approaches in studying the allocation of resources within households. The primary research aims of the project were two-fold. First, it was designed to identify the allocative systems that exist within households through studying the values, attitudes, beliefs and behaviours of household members. Secondly, it was intended to lead to the design and pre-test of a short questionnaire module for possible use in the BHPS questionnaire schedule. In using qualitative research techniques both to identify key indicators and to clarify concepts prior to a much more extensive quantitative project, this project is not unusual. However, in another respect it is unusual. Although it has drawn extensively on the qualitative data to inform the design and construction of the questionnaire component to be used in the survey, it has also attempted to maintain the integrity of the qualitative data in its own right.

Since many of the epistemological issues raised by linking qualitative and quantitative [1] approaches have been discussed earlier in the volume, it is not my intention to explore these in detail here. Rather, I will concentrate on the research process itself and the implications of using multiple research methodologies and techniques in a mutually informative way in designing and carrying out social research in the field. The process of data collection will be examined in relation to the practical considerations faced by the research team; and the linkage between the qualitative and quantitative phases of the research will be explored. The difficulties posed by practical constraints on the design of the questionnaire to be used by the BHPS in the quantitative phase of the research will also be covered. In addition, the qualitative data will be used to illustrate the ways in which using multiple data collection methods allowed clarification of the theoretical and conceptual framework with which we entered the field at the outset of the qualitative phase. The significance of this process for the development of the BHPS questionnaire component will be examined.

The research setting

In 1989 the Economic and Social Research Council (ESRC) established the Research Centre on Micro-Social Change in Britain at the University of Essex. The main task of the Research Centre is to conduct the British Household Panel Study (BHPS), a ten year panel survey of a nationally representative sample of 5000 British households. The sample will be drawn from the Postcode Address File, with every adult aged 16 or over found at those addresses being included in the sample. In all, this is expected to yield a sample of some 10,000 individuals in a range of household circumstances from the single person household to multi-adult situations. The BHPS will annually interview every adult member of the 5,000 households using a structured questionnaire as the main data collection instrument. The questionnaire will consist of a core element covering a broad range of issues including income, labour market behaviour, housing conditions, household composition, education, health, economic decision making in the household, residential mobility, and socio-economic values. There will also be a variable component which will focus on different issues each year. Each sample member will be followed throughout the life of the panel and, as the children of sample members reach the age of 16, they will become part of the sample. Adult members who form new households will be followed and members of these households incorporated into the study.

The major objective of the BHPS is to provide longitudinal data for the study of social change. Given the size and representativeness of the sample, the BHPS data will predominantly be used for quantitative analyses which aim to make statistical inferences which can be generalized to the population as a whole. The information will be collected at the level of the individual, allowing the links between both individual and household situation as well as those with the wider social and economic environment to be explored. The researcher will be able to choose the unit and level of analysis appropriate to their research objectives, although the data collected through the structured questionnaire schedule will be most amenable to quantitative rather than qualitative forms of analysis.

The panel study will collect continuous data on income and employment by carrying out relatively detailed income and employment histories covering the year between interviews. Other areas of the schedule however, will be limited to collecting information on the respondent's current situation at the point of interview. What is initially clear is that the quantitative data set will allow change to be analyzed as a sequence of events or observed 'outcomes' measured at yearly intervals. The major advantage of longitudinal rather than cross-sectional data, is that it enables the researcher to establish the temporal ordering of events. However, although making inferences about the direction and causality of change will be possible, this form of analysis will tell us little about the process through which change occurs. Motivation, meaning and definitions of events and relationships play a central role in determining social action. Shifts in perception and motivation often occur in a subtle and diffuse manner, not always tied to particular events. In addition, change may not be experienced by individuals as occurring at one point in time but as part of an interconnected sequence of events. Collecting information on these more nebulous social processes is problematic even within a qualitative methodological framework. But when attempting to operationalize standardized indicators in a quantitative context, the difficulties increase. These processes are simply not accessible to the researcher in the context of a structured questionnaire and remain more easily explored in an interpretative analysis of qualitative data.

For the researcher using a longitudinal data set such as the BHPS, two main issues are involved. First there is the type of longitudinal data collected; second, there is the type of analysis allowed by the data. In the case of the BHPS, although continuous employment and income data will be collected, the data on resource allocation will be restricted to 'current state' at the point of interview. While it is recognized that the ideal would be to collect continuous data in all areas covered by the questionnaire it would not be feasible to do so without imposing an intolerably heavy burden on both the respondents and the study. Secondly, focusing on a series of observed 'outcomes' does not, for example, allow the analysis of ongoing, decision-making processes within the household. As the chapter will show, clear-cut decisions about resource allocation within households are rare. In the context of a qualitative, depth interview, people talk in terms of their financial arrangements 'evolving' in response to changing circumstances. The assumption that people make clearly identifiable decisions is therefore problematic in cases where the decision-making process is perceived as seamless over time. As has been noted, it is the subjective interpretation of events and social processes which are not easily measured in the context of a structured questionnaire. Where concern is with the explanation of why change occurs, drawing conclusions about the causality of change may therefore prove to be misleading if based on a series of observed 'outcomes' alone (Laurie and Sullivan, 1991).

In part, the tension between quantitative and qualitative approaches arises out of the differing definitions of 'explanation' employed in the respective analysis techniques. The logic of quantitative analysis relies predominantly on the statistical method in which hypotheses are tested on the data and inferences made from the sample to the population under study. Qualitative analysis most commonly uses the technique of analytic induction in which the researcher moves from the data, through the formulation of hypotheses, and sometimes to their testing and verification. While, as Hammersley argues (Chapter 2), this logical distinction is often an oversimplification of research practice, there remains a marked distinction between statistical and analytic inductive approaches. In broad terms, 'explanation' in much quantitative analysis involves correlational associations between variables and, in a multi-variate analysis, includes the process of controlling for the effects of prior and intervening variables. In qualitative analysis 'explanation' is an interpretative exercise concerned not only with understanding the 'variable' itself but also the relationship between 'variables'. For the quantitative analyst, variables are treated as being unproblematically given by the data. For the qualitative analyst however, it is the 'variable' itself which becomes problematized and in need of explanation. In order to combine quantitative and qualitative approaches in analysis Fielding and Fielding (1986,p.17) argue that '.....we could take the variable-centred regularities but would regard them not as an "explanation" but as "social facts" for explanation.' In this way, the qualitative data would not, as so often occurs, be 'added on' to the quantitative data as illustration. A further research strategy which the Research Centre recognizes would be valuable in order to alleviate problems of this kind, would be to encourage the setting up of qualitative projects in tandem with the main survey. The qualitative and quantitative data could then be used comparatively in analysis to provide findings which were on the one hand statistically reliable, and on the other allowing a depth of interpretation that would not be possible from the quantitative data alone.

The Household Allocative Systems Project

As has been discussed in Chapter 1, research is a social and political process as well as a methodological and technical one. Practical and political constraints, and theoretical and research paradigms all influence both the choice of methodology and the practice of the research itself. One influential aspect of the environment in which research is carried out is the methodological experience and preferences of the researchers involved. In the case of the Household Allocative Systems Project, three of the researchers (based at the Research Centre) were involved in the design of the qualitative project and the collection of the data. The principal investigator has extensive experience of quantitative research but little direct experience of qualitative methods of research, with a long-standing interest in social class. My own interest is in using multiple methods in the investigation of social processes with my substantive interest being the determinants of women's labour market participation. The third researcher in the team has extensive experience of qualitative methods and was firmly committed to this approach. In addition to the Centre researchers, an external research agency, Social and Community Planning Research (SCPR), was involved in the first stage of the project. At regular meetings throughout the fieldwork, interviewers were briefed jointly by Centre and agency researchers and the interviewers' accounts of how the fieldwork was progressing were continuously monitored. This process added considerably to the amount of consultation involved but also generated many ideas and further lines of enquiry to pursue. Despite the positive aspect of utilizing a number of researchers' skills, the sheer number of people and spread of methodological preferences undoubtedly led to tensions at various stages. However, it also provided a means of internally regulating the research process since there was always someone ready to point out the limitations or potential of what was being proposed at any given time. At times, consensus could not be achieved and the research process was a constant exchange of competing views. Issues were reiterated from a number of differing perspectives, with some remaining problematic throughout.

Multiple methods and techniques

The Household Allocative Systems Project was carried out in two main stages. The first stage consisted of unstructured qualitative interviews, group discussions, and the pre-test of the structured questionnaire component. The second stage consisted of further unstructured qualitative interviews and group discussions with members of multi-adult households. The final design work and testing of the component to be carried in the BHPS questionnaire schedule was carried out in the months following the Household Allocative Systems Project.

The qualitative interviews and group discussions were explicitly concerned to collect information not only on the distribution, management and control of financial resources but also on the domestic division of labour, the allocation of time and space, and access to consumer goods and durables which (nominally) belong to all household members. It was also recognized that a satisfactory analysis would include not only intra- but also inter-household transfers of resources, whether in monetary form or in the exchange of care or labour. Further, given the longitudinal design of the BHPS, we needed to gain as much information as possible on whether households reported altering their internal organization in response to life events or changes in, for example, household composition, health or employment status. In terms of designing the structured questions it was important to operationalize the indicators most likely to be sensitive to change.

The first stage of the project was carried out in cooperation with SCPR. In-depth interviews were carried out with nineteen married or cohabiting couples, each interviewed separately, and seven group discussions, consisting of eight to ten people each. Only one member of each couple selected participated in a group discussion. A total of seventy-seven households were covered, using a quota sample to ensure a range of socio-economic and demographic characteristics. A short screening questionnaire was used to select respondents although a few were found through snowballing. Since one of the major research aims of the project was to collect information on the management of finances within the household, and independent financial management between partners is the most unusual form of organization, it was necessary to boost the number of these households. Snowballing to find these couples was therefore a pragmatic response to our research needs which aimed to cover as broad a spectrum of financial arrangements as possible.

In the first stage the sample consisted of fifty-one men and forty-five women with ages ranging from seventeen to seventy-four, although there was a bias towards the younger age groups. In part, this was due to a decision to use some of the group discussions for people under twenty-five years old in order to gain information on the formation of new households and their internal organization. Although we recognized that ethnicity would be likely to have a considerable impact on the internal organization of the household, it was decided that within the limits of this project, we would be unable to explore fully the cultural differences which may be present. (This remains an area for future research.) The sample represented a variety of household types, about half with dependent children and a small number of the group participants coming from multi-generational households. We were particularly keen to ensure that not only middle-income households were included, but also that the extremes of the income range were represented. Even though our aim was not to provide a representative sample, we did attempt to construct an unbiased sample in this regard. The fact that a sample is not statistically representative of a population does not imply that bias is unimportant in a qualitative context. Through unwittingly excluding sections of the population under study, a qualitative study is equally prone to the effects of bias which may produce spurious findings. The individual incomes of respondents ranged from less than £4,000 per annum to over £50,000. Of the nineteen households in which both partners were interviewed, eight were dual-earner households, five single-earner households and in six both were living on benefits or pensions. In the discussion groups seven people came from households living solely on benefits or pensions and the remainder from a mixture of single and dual-earner households.

As noted earlier, the qualitative interviews and group discussions were designed to lead to the development of a short questionnaire module to be pre-tested for inclusion within the BHPS questionnaire. The resulting pre-test module was designed and administered to twenty individuals along with a 'test and check' module to try and determine where there were difficulties with specific questions. The sample for the pre-test was once again a quota sample but was drawn from among the participants in the group discussions. Although there was some concern that this could lead to conditioning effects, it was judged that the context would be sufficiently different from the group discussions to avoid any serious bias. In addition, there was a lapse of some three or four months between the two interview points. The major advantage of this approach was that we already had a considerable amount of information about the respondents and their households, which allowed us to select a sample based on detailed information concerning the internal organization of their households. We also had data on a broad range of these households' socio-demographic characteristics. In the context of a small pre-test, the concern was not with the representativeness of the sample but rather with the issue of inclusiveness, namely all the types of households and methods of allocation so far encountered in the project.

The fieldwork, including the individual interviews, the group discussions and the pre-test, was carried out in two geographical locations, one in the north of England and the other in the south-east. All the interviews and group discussions were conducted on an informal basis and lasted up to two hours. An outline topic guide was used to assist interviewers in both the individual interviews and group discussions. All proceedings were tape recorded for later transcription and analysis. While producing comparable data, we found that each technique was suited to the exploration of different aspects of resource allocation. The individual interviews were able to obtain more detailed information on the distribution, management, control and use of household resources than was possible in the context of the group discussions. The strength of the group discussions was that they enabled fuller exploration of the attitudes and values underlying different methods of household organization. We found that the dynamics of the group encouraged greater frankness than in the individual interviews, with the dynamics of each group shifting in accordance with its composition. Being part of a group seemed to have the effect of encouraging people to express themselves more freely. This was apparent, for example, where individuals were reticent about voicing what they perceived as criticisms of their partners' attitudes or behaviour. The more forthcoming members of the group would actively encourage the more reserved members to speak openly about their relationship with their partners. In the context of a group of strangers it became socially acceptable to voice opinions which it may have been unacceptable to voice within the respondent's own circle of friends and family, or in the interview situation within the conjugal home. As Morgan suggests, we explicitly used 'the group interaction to produce data and insights that would be less accessible without the interaction found in a group.' (Morgan,1988, p.12)

The second stage of the research used qualitative methods and focused on three-generational households and households where adult children were present. This stage was carried out in Colchester and consisted of two group discussions of eight people each and individual, depth interviews with all members of six three-generational households, covering a total of twenty-two households. The primary purpose of this stage was to assess whether there were any significant variations in multi-adult households to be taken into account in the design of the BHPS questionnaire component. Beyond this, these interviews provided some fascinating material which indicates the diversity of experience within the same type of households structure.

As we were specifically interested in multi-adult and three-generational households we used the electoral register to identify households with four or more members. In addition, in order to avoid households of unrelated single adults sharing accommodation, only households in which at least two people shared the same surname were selected. The problem with using the electoral register for our purpose was that we had no way of knowing the relationships between people in these households or their ages (except in the case of those about to turn eighteen) or, indeed, whether they were all permanently resident at the address given on the register. Therefore we decided to use a short postal screening questionnaire in order to establish contact with and make final selection of households for interview. This was done on the basis of household composition and the relationships of the people within them. The majority of households contacted consisted of families with young adult children still living in the parental home and individuals from sixteen of these households were selected for the group discussions. It was decided to have one group discussion with parents of young adult children still living in the parental home and the second with young adults living in the parental home. Only one member of each household took part and none of the participants were related in any way. All members of the three-generational households selected were interviewed individually.

The logistics of interviewing every member of these large households was in itself relevant to the design of the BHPS where interviewers are required to try and gain the cooperation of all household members. Of course, we had the advantage of having already gained consent to be interviewed from some members of the household. We discovered that once personal contact had been established in the household, reluctant members were persuaded to take part. In a household of seven or eight people, all with differing work schedules and times at which they would be available for interview, several visits were often necessary to complete the interviews. Perhaps not surprisingly, it was the young adults who were most difficult to find [2]. Paying a number of visits did, however, have the advantage of increasing the trust of the families, as the researcher became a familiar visitor to the home. It also allowed some limited observation of household routines and interaction between household members, information which can be incorporated into the analysis of qualitative interview and discussion group data. In the context of a formal interview setting using a structured questionnaire, this directly observed information is not recorded and is therefore unavailable to the analyst.

Perhaps inevitably, the dual purposes of the project created certain tensions between the data produced by the qualitative component and the design constraints imposed by the quantitative component. Tension became particularly evident during the design of the questions for the BHPS survey schedule. While all the data from the qualitative work testified to the complexity of arrangements within the household, the segment of the forty-five minute BHPS questionnaire schedule, which was to be used for questions on resource distribution within the household, was allowed only five minutes of interviewing time. So, beyond the technical constraints of the survey instrument itself, we were faced with a major time constraint. In practice, it was decided to restrict the BHPS survey questions to the domestic division of labour and internal and external financial transfers.

Theoretical perspectives

A number of different approaches have been adopted in the study of resource allocation within the household. For sociologists, much of the work was initially stimulated by feminist researchers. The theoretical interest of this research focuses on the gendered nature of relations of power and authority within the conjugal unit. One area which has attracted attention is money. Jan Pahl was among the first to trace flows of money within the household as a means of looking at power within the marital relationship (1980, 1983, 1988, 1989, 1990). Pahl used qualitative methods in order to identify patterns of money management and developed a taxonomy of 'household allocative systems'. These are:

Whole Wage System: one person, usually the woman, is responsible for managing all household expenditure.
Allowance System: partners have defined spheres of responsibility for expenditure with, usually, the woman being given 'housekeeping' money.
Shared Management:
a) Common pool: both partners have access to all income and share responsibilities for all expenditure decisions.
b) Partial pool: both partners put some proportion of their earnings into the common pool and use retentions for personal spending money.
Independent Management: partners keep their incomes separate and each is responsible for different items of expenditure.

Lydia Morris (1988, 1989, 1990) uses Pahl's taxonomy to examine not only social and economic relationships within the household, but the links with the broader social and economic environment in which they are situated. For example, she examines women's labour market participation through an analysis of the constraints and possibilities offered by their household circumstances and the effect of male unemployment on the internal organization of households. Pahl's taxonomy has been applied in a quantitative context by the ESRC Social Change and Economic Life Initiative (SCELI), which drew its sample from six local labour markets in Britain. SCELI collected information on financial arrangements between married or cohabiting couples, so providing the first large-scale quantitative data set on this topic. Pahl's systems were summarized in a series of descriptive statements and respondents were asked to assess which statement was closest to their own household allocative system. Together with a question on who has the 'final say' on major financial decisions, these data were coded according to Pahl's taxonomy (Vogler, 1990).
Social policy researchers and economists have contributed to this debate from a slightly different perspective. The former have provided

a powerful critique of taxation and benefit policies which assume equal access to and benefit from resources entering the household (see, for example, Glendinning and Millar, 1987; Brannen and Moss, 1987; Wilson, 1987a). For economists, the measurement of income at an individual rather than household level has been a concern (see, for example, Jenkins, 1989, on poverty). In addition, issues of labour supply have been addressed by economists who have seen the differential patterns of labour market participation of men and women as the consequence of the rational deployment of household resources and human capital returns in the public and private spheres (see, for example, Becker, 1981). These sociological, social policy and economic approaches, while having points of convergence, tend to focus on different aspects of the same phenomena and each requires specific types of data.

With the exception of SCELI, most research into the allocation of resources within households has taken place within the context of relatively small projects, using predominantly qualitative methodological approaches. The collection of data on resource allocation in the context of a survey using a structured questionnaire, is therefore relatively untested. Initially, the theoretical approach adopted by the Household Allocative Systems Project followed that of Pahl and SCELI. However, given that the BHPS would be interviewing every member of the sampled households, the extent to which it should maintain an exclusive focus on married and cohabiting couples soon became an issue. In order to gain any indication of both household and individual welfare the view that it would be necessary to collect information concerning financial transfers between all household members gradually emerged. Two specific issues had to be addressed. First, we were concerned with the theoretical justification for broadening our approach to include other household members, and second with the more practical concerns of how we could best collect this type of data within the context of a structured questionnaire. There was little helpful existing research to guide us and theoretical perspectives remained underdeveloped. However, multi-generational households are of particular interest and significance when examining social relationships based on financial, physical or emotional dependence, obligation, or familial duty. These are issues of direct policy relevance since the provision of informal care for elderly or sick relatives within the family home is likely to attract increasing attention over the coming decade as the proportion of elderly people in the population rises. In addition, there has been a growing interest in inter-generational transfers of financial resources, in particular the economic support provided by the older generation for their adult children (see, for example, Cheal, 1983, 1987, 1988, 1989). For households composed of unrelated adults sharing accommodation, we hypothesised that the financial arrangements would be more likely to be purely pragmatic and not mediated by emotional commitments of the same order as familial households.

The issue of whether to broaden our approach to include all household members was to some extent resolved by the qualitative interviews with couples. In several cases we found it difficult to examine the domestic and financial arrangements between partners to the exclusion of other household members. This was particularly clear in three-generational households where we believed that the information we were gaining from the middle-generation couple was providing an incomplete picture of the complexity of relationships within the household. By focusing on the 'simplifying case' of the couple we were eliciting a partial account which allowed no means of assessing the mechanisms through which resource allocation was mediated by different relationships within the household. For example, in one case where an elderly mother relied on her daughter-in-law for continuous care, in return the mother was obliged by her son to pass complete control of her finances to him. Even though the elderly mother clearly resented this situation, she remained powerless to alter it. While it is arguable that the existing theoretical approaches concerning power and patriarchy are justified in concentrating on the couple alone, it is also clear that where interest is in intra-household resource allocation , a broader perspective must be taken. In the context of the design of the BHPS where the intention is to follow changing household circumstances, the justification for incorporating all household members is stronger still. These considerations led to the decision to conduct the second stage of the project in which qualitative interviews and group discussions were carried out with members of some multi-adult households.

Conceptual clarification

One of the major advantages of our qualitative data was that it enabled conceptual clarification. It has been argued that the use of analytic induction is a technique which 'forces the sociologist to formulate and state his (her) theories in such a way as to indicate crucial tests of the theory and to permit the explicit search for negative cases' (Denzin, 1970 p.197). Through a process of examining each negative case, redefining the phenomenon, and reformulating the hypotheses, researchers can test their theories and try to make propositions which hold across all the data. While the analytic process may not be as clear cut as Denzin's account suggests, we did find however, that it was the negative cases which were in many ways the most revealing as they indicated the shortcomings of our conceptual framework.

As I noted earlier, we entered the field with a conceptual framework derived from the work of Jan Pahl. Each 'household allocative system' describes the arrangements made by spouses for managing their money and identifies which member of the couple controls the distribution of income within the household. A distinction is drawn between the management and control of household funds: on the one hand spheres of responsibility in relation to spending patterns and the domestic division of labour, and, on the other, who, within the relationship has the final say on financial matters. For Pahl, the decision-making process is a crucial indicator of power within marriage, with the dominant partner in decision making being the partner most likely to control household funds.

While Pahl's categories have provided some major insights into the internal workings of the household, we found a number of unresolved difficulties with the model. Some of these relate to problems which are inherent in any classification system (Laurie and Sullivan, 1991) and others to the complexity of the processes being categorized. We found that the model assumes that two, three or four features will coexist within any one system. The shared management system, for example, assumes that both partners have access to household income, and are jointly responsible for both the management of household income and for expenditure from a shared pool of money. This presents a measurement problem, since in reality many situations are not so clear cut. The presence of overlapping characteristics or the absence of expected features makes the unambiguous assignation of observations to categories difficult (Ritchie and Thomas, 1990, p.9). For example, in the case of one couple we interviewed, the husband had a full-time job with his whole salary being paid into a joint bank account to pay the mortgage, bills and general household spending. The wife had two part-time jobs and received child benefit for their two children. One of her wages was transferred to the joint account for household spending. The second wage and the child benefit were kept separately by the wife for large bills, holidays and 'luxuries'. It is unclear whether this arrangement falls into the allowance, partial pool or common pool system. In another case, where three generations were present, the middle-generation couple had distinct spheres of responsibility for household expenditure, the husband paying the mortgage and the bills and the wife paying for food and household items. The husband gave a proportion of his earnings to his wife for housekeeping and kept the remainder for household bills and personal spending. The husband's mother gave part of her pension and all of her attendance allowance to the wife who used this money for housekeeping and personal spending. The seventeen year old daughter paid ten pounds per week to her mother who saved this for large items of household expenditure. Once again it is unclear whether this arrangement falls into the allowance or partial pooling category, with the added complication of how to cope with the contributions made by the elderly mother and adult daughter. In all we found that of the nineteen couples interviewed individually only four (three with a common pool and one with an independent management system) could unambiguously be assigned to one category. Another two (one with an independent management and one with a common pool system) could be assigned if the category was broadly interpreted. In the remaining thirteen cases there were either significant features of a category missing or there was no appropriate category at all (Ritchie and Thomas, 1990, p.3).

The most problematic category of the taxonomy is that of shared management or 'pooling'. This presents problems of measurement in two respects. First, the meaning of the term 'pooling' is by no means consistently understood by respondents. In the depth interviews and group discussions we found that it was a term commonly used by people to describe their financial arrangements as in some way shared. In this context the term did not appear to be problematic, possibly due to the fact that it was disguised by the amount of detailed information we were collecting. However, in the pre-test of the questionnaire component where the term 'pooling' was used in the structured questions, it emerged as extremely problematic. Respondents were asked what the term 'pooling' actually meant to them after the questionnaire had been administered. We found that 'pooling' was interpreted in diverse ways: (1) putting cash together to pay for food or to go shopping; (2) having a joint bank account, even if resourced and accessed by one partner only; (3) having a 'household purse' even if only one income went into it; and (4) putting cheques together to pay a bill (Ritchie and Thomas,

1990, p.7). The only cases where the term 'pooling' was interpreted as we expected was either where there was no merging of money at all or, in contrast, where there was only one joint bank account into which both incomes were immediately paid. The different results produced by the different methods suggest that analytically the concept of 'pooling' is problematic.

Secondly, it is on the topic of money and marriage that respondents are most likely to respond in ideological terms, reflecting normative expectations about the way marriage should be conducted (Wilson, 1987b). In other words, the tendency is to report financial arrangements which present the marriage as an equal partnership. Interestingly, the SCELI data show that men are slightly more likely to accentuate the degree of sharing, perhaps as a reaction against being seen as the dominant partner (Vogler, 1990, p.10). For many people sharing and trust are the fundamental principles upon which marriage and coupledom ought to be based. As one woman participant in a group discussion described her feelings about money and marriage:

> I've just always thought it's shared, you know, it wouldn't have crossed my mind to have my money and he to have his separately, it's just all shared... I couldn't imagine a marriage any other way.

However, at another point in the discussion the same woman described her financial relationship with her husband in the following way:

> Everything is joint but I have my own account that I had when I was at work and my husband pays in money for Sainsbury's and everything, so he says that's his way of keeping some hold on me, because with a cheque book I'm dangerous so he tends to hold on. Although it's in joint names and I can use it if I need to, he tends to sort of look after it more than me. But I do have my own account.

From this woman's perspective, it is clear that control of the household finances is not equally shared but ultimately rests with the husband even though the ideological commitment is to equality in financial arrangements. This situation was by no means uncommon in both in-depth individual interviews and group discussions, but sorting out ambiguities of this type remains problematic when collecting data with a structured questionnaire. Consequently, we decided that using the

Pahl categories alone would not be sufficient for classifying methods of financial allocation from the BHPS questionnaire. It was decided that additional measures of income flows and transfers between household members and information on individual access to household funds should also be collected.

In the analysis of the qualitative data it became apparent that access to resources which nominally belong to all household members is often mediated by gatekeeping procedures. In many cases these were achieved through limiting access to bank accounts, whether these were held in joint names or not. In terms of the development of the BHPS questionnaire it was clear that if we were to use the existence of a joint bank account as an indicator of jointness or sharing between household members, we would be in danger of producing spurious results unless we asked an additional question to establish who controlled the use of accounts held in joint names. Given the time and space constraints we were working to in the design of the questionnaire, we were aware that we would be unable to collect information on all the means used to hold or save money. For example, money kept in cash in purses, boxes, tins and so on would be impossible to cover. While we had encountered a variety of means for holding money the trend for those in employment is increasingly towards payment of salaries directly into bank accounts and we found only a minority of households with no bank account. This led us to the view that questions on bank accounts would be the most useful to include. These would provide a more objective measure than the self-assessment question on household allocative systems alone, as well as providing us with some factual information for comparison.

What emerges clearly from the qualitative data is that each member of the household legitimates their claim to household funds through the use to which they are put. The legitimate use of household funds is intimately connected with the gendering of spheres of responsibility for household spending. For women in particular, their labour market status strongly influences which items of expenditure they consider to be legitimate. Women who are dependent upon a sole main earner feel that they have the least legitimate claim to use money entering the household for anything which is not defined as 'household expenditure'. This was most evident in women's attitudes to spending money on themselves rather than on the household, their children, husbands or partners. Many women expressed considerable guilt about spending on clothes or activities for themselves since they defined this personal expenditure as unnecessary or extravagant. Some women resorted to strategies such as hiding a new dress in the wardrobe for a few weeks and then quite truthfully saying they had bought it some time ago. Alternatively, they would automatically lower the price of the item bought when their partners enquired about the cost. Where women were earning and making a contribution to the cost of running the household, these feelings of guilt were less salient. However, for many women the motivation to enter paid employment was not only to earn their 'own' money, but to pay for household costs. Women with no independent income were more likely to express feelings of guilt not only about personal spending but also about the fact that they were not contributing to the household costs. By defining spending on themselves as illegitimate, their feelings about being a 'burden' were to some extent assuaged. Many women saw spending time or money on purely personal items or activities as not only wasteful but also selfish. One woman taking an Open University course described her feelings as follows:

I do the O.U. and I get a bit guilty about spending nineteen pounds a month just for me on the O.U. ....because it's not cheap. It's not just that, I know why I feel guilty. I feel guilty because it takes time off the family as well and you're never quite free of your responsibilities as a mother and a wife...

Many men expressed the view that the price their wives paid for not working was to take on full responsibility for domestic tasks and it was a 'fair' arrangement which their wives had entered into through 'choice'. One man participating in a group discussion described his wife as a 'diamond' since she sacrificed herself to the needs of her husband and children. When it was suggested to him by another member of the group that she may not be happy with her situation his response was:

Well, we don't have that problem, thank God, because my wife I think has accepted that's her role you see...I don't think she actually shows that she's upset or she wants a break or anything, she's quite contented, it appears that way anyway.

Another man expressed the view that, while being the main earner did not necessarily give him the right to expect his wife to carry the full domestic load he did feel that it...

...justifies your laziness. Now that isn't to say in our household we don't try and share things...but at the end of the day I do mentally think, you know, that's your problem, you know, get on with it sort of thing. That's horrible isn't it? But it's true.

It was evident from the qualitative data that we had to attempt to design some questions for the BHPS survey that would tap the extent to which, particularly in the couple situation, each partner felt able to spend on items of personal expenditure without being accountable to their partner. Given the complexity of the processes of negotiation occurring within the household, it would be impossible to achieve a full account within the time constraints of the BHPS schedule. However, it was decided that minimal information on amounts of personal spending money and degree of accountability to partner must be collected.

The information from households with young adult children present pointed to further complexities. Where adult children in paid employment were present we found that they usually contributed something towards the expenses of the household. This took the form of 'board' or 'keep' money with the amount paid negotiated between parents and adult children. The amount contributed varied both within and between households and appeared to be arrived at on the basis of the wage level of the child and the total household income level. Where several children are contributing, household income can increase significantly even though we found that individual amounts were never very large. Individual payments usually fell somewhere between ten and twenty-five pounds per week, and were generally considered to be a contribution towards food, rent and household bills. On an individual basis the adult child who remains within the parental home benefits from the comparatively low cost of living. Indeed, the inability to afford separate accommodation was cited by many young people as a major reason for remaining within the parental home. The move from being a dependent child who contributes nothing to household costs to the status of a contributing 'adult' was not totally related to age but also to employment status and wage level. Those in full-time education living on a grant were generally not expected to pay anything but those receiving unemployment benefit were expected to pay a minimal token amount. In higher income households it seemed to be important to parents that their children were aware of their financial responsibilities once they were earning a wage. Insisting on a contribution of some kind was seen as a means of doing this. In the case of low income households or those with a number of adult children present it was of course also a necessity to maintain the household's standard of living. (While it would be reasonable to expect some cultural variation on these issues, we had no means of exploring these with our respondents). In three generational households the arrangements were even more complex. Money passed between household members not only as payment for food and bills but also for personal spending needs or temporary loans. Control over the income of elderly dependents emerged as an issue which remains to be explored in future research as increasing numbers of elderly people come to rely on relatives for their care.

In terms of the BHPS questionnaire, we concluded that the qualitative data from the second stage justified taking the broader view and collecting information on transfers of money between all household members including the use to which that money was put. Questions about the domestic division of labour were also designed to include all household members, enabling analysis of not only gendered spheres of responsibility within couple relationships but also the contribution of unpaid labour made by other household members. There was little possibility of exploring people's feelings about financial transfers within the BHPS questionnaire, but the qualitative data provided us with some insights into the types of arrangements we are likely to encounter in complex households in the panel survey itself. This will allow us to approach the analysis of the quantitative data with a greater understanding than would otherwise have been possible.

Conclusion

In practice, the use of multiple methods and research techniques has proved both difficult and enlightening. Their application to the same substantive area is challenging to both existing theoretical approaches and methodological presumptions. By using multiple methods to gather data many of the arguments which assert a necessary link between theoretical perspective and method of data collection tend to be overtaken by what Burgess has called 'methodological pragmatism'(1982, p.163). Despite this, self-defined quantitative and qualitative researchers approach the collection and analysis of data from very different perspectives. Whether or not the 'logical separation' between methods is maintained in the practice of social research may be of secondary importance. If researchers assert that they are adhering to a specific logical framework this will influence their choice of data collection and analysis techniques, often placing arbitrary restrictions on the research. In the case of our project, we began with a set of research aims which expanded and developed through the course of the research. Issues and questions emerged from the data collected in the first stage of the project which we felt obliged to pursue, not only for clarification of the qualitative data but to meet the design imperatives of a quantitative, longitudinal household study. Without the use of qualitative methods which allowed the detailed exploration of intra-household resource allocation, it is doubtful that many of these issues would have emerged. Although the aim of designing the questionnaire module remained unaltered throughout, the use of multiple methods enabled the scope of the questions designed for the BHPS schedule to be far broader than initially envisaged. However, the difficulties we faced in designing questions within the restricted time available for questions on household resource allocation in the survey schedule, should be noted. It was not the technical difficulties of designing standardized questions which posed the greatest problems but the limited amount of space available in the BHPS questionnaire for questions on this topic. The issue was therefore not one of attempting to reconcile competing epistemological perspectives but of practical design constraints and possibilities.

Notes

1.   Although the difference between methodologies tends to be artificially exaggerated by counterposing 'qualitative' against 'quantitative', I use this terminology in recognition of the epistemological distinction between methodologies derived from interpretivist and positivist philosophical traditions.

2.   In relation to BHPS fieldwork practices, this pointed to the need to brief interviewers on the importance of gaining complete rather than partial household interviews which could be biased in favour of older household members.

Acknowledgements

Acknowledgements to Julia Brannen, Oriel Sullivan, Jean Duncombe, David Rose and members of the BHPS Research Group.

166   *Mixing Methods: qualitative and quantitative research*

The support of the Economic and Social Research Council (ESRC) is also gratefully acknowledged. The work was part of the programme of the ESRC Research Centre on Micro-Social Change in Britain.

References

Becker, G.S.(1981) *A Treatise on the Family*. Cambridge, Massachussetts: Harvard University Press.

Brannen, J. and Moss, P. (1987) 'Dual earner households: Women's financial contributions after the birth of the first child.' In J. Brannen and G. Wilson (eds) *Give and Take in Families*. London: Allen and Unwin.

Bryman, A. (1984) 'The debate about quantitative and qualitative research: A question of method or epistemology?' *The British Journal of Sociology, 35*, 1, pp.75-92

Bryman, A. (1988) *Quantity and Quality in Social Research*. London: Unwin Hyman.

Burgess, R.G. (ed.) (1982) *Field Research: A Sourcebook and Field Manual*. London: George Allen and Unwin.

Cheal, D. (1983) 'Intergenerational family transfers.' *Journal of Marriage and the Family November*, pp.805-813.

Cheal, D. (1987) 'Intergenerational transfers and life course management: Towards a socio-economic perspective.' In A. Bryman, B. Bytheway, P. Allatt and T. Keil (eds) *Rethinking the Life Cycle*. London: Macmillan.

Cheal, D. (1988) 'Theories of serial flow in intergenerational transfers.' *International Journal of Aging and Human Development, 26*, 4.

Cheal, D. (1989) A Value-Added Model of the Household Economy. Paper presented at B.S.A. Conference, Plymouth.

Denzin, N.K. (1970) *The Research Act in Sociology*. London: Butterworth.

Denzin, N.K. (1978) *The Research Act 2nd.edition*. McGraw-Hill Book Company, USA.

Edwards, M. (1982) 'Financial arrangements made by husbands and wives: Findings of a survey.' *Australian and New Zealand Journal of Sociology, 18*, 3.

Edwards, M. (1984) Financial arrangements within families. *Social Security Journal*. Australian Government Publishing Service.

Fielding, N.G.and Fielding, J.L.(1986) *Linking Data: Qualitative Research Methods Series, Vol.4*. California: Sage.

Glendinning, C.and Millar, J.(eds) (1987) *Women and Poverty in Britain*. Hemel Hempstead: Wheatsheaf Books.

Jenkins, S.P.(1989) Poverty Measurement and the Within-Household Distribution. Mimeo, ESRC Workshop on Changing Definitions of Poverty, London: PSI.

Laurie, H. and Sullivan, O. (1991) 'Combining qualitative and quantitative data in the longitudinal Study of household allocations.' *Sociological Review, 39*, 1, pp.113-130.

Morgan, D.L. (1988) *Focus Groups as Qualitative Research* Qualitative Research Methods Series, Vol.16, Sage Publications, USA.

Morris, L. (1988) 'Employment, the household and social networks.' In D. Gallie (ed.) *Employment in Britain*. Oxford: Blackwell.

Morris, L. (1989) 'Household strategies, the individual, the collectivity and the labour market: The case of married couples.' *Work, Employment and Society, 3*, 4, pp.447-464.

Morris, L. (1990) *The Workings of the Household: A US-UK comparison*. Family Life Series. Cambridge: Polity Press.

Morris, L. with Ruane, S.(1989) *Household Finance Management and the Labour Market*. Aldershot: Gower.

Pahl, J. (1980) 'Patterns of money management within marriage.' *Journal of Social Policy, 9*, 3, pp.313-335.

Pahl, J. (1983) 'The allocation of money and the structuring of inequality within marriage.' *Sociological Review, 31*, 2, pp.237-262.

Pahl, J. (1988) 'Making ends meet: Earning, sharing, spending: Married couples and their money.' In R. Walker and G. Parker (eds) *Money Matters*. London: Sage.

Pahl, J. (1989) *Money and Marriage*. London: Macmillan.

Pahl, J. (1990) 'Household spending, personal spending and the control of money in marriage.' *Sociology, 24*, pp.119-138.

Ritchie, J. and Thomas, A. (1990) Household allocative systems: A working paper on the definition and description of household allocative systems. London: Social and Community Planning Research.

Vogler, C.(1989) Labour market change and patterns of financial allocation within households. *Working Paper 12*, The Economic and Social Research Council, The Social Change and Economic Life Initiative, Nuffield College, Oxford.

Wilson, G. (1987a) *Women and Money:The Distribution of Resources and Responsibilities in the Family*. Aldershot: Gower.

Wilson, G.(1987b) 'Money: Patterns of responsibility and irresponsibility in marriage.' In J. Brannen and G. Wilson (eds) *Give and Take in Families.* London: Allen and Unwin.

Index